CONNECTING THE DOTS: ACROSS LEARNING SUPPORT HIGHER EDUCATION TO ENHANCE STUDENT LEARNING

EDITORS

MICHELLE SCHNEIDER

JADE KELSALL

HELEN WEBSTER

Connecting the dots: Collaboration across learning support professions in higher education to enhance student learning

Editors: Michelle Schneider; Jade Kelsall; Dr Helen Webster

ISBN paperback: 9780957665262

ISBN e-book: 9780957665286

Copyright © 2015

All rights reserved.

No part of this book can be reproduced in any form or by written, electronic or mechanical, including photocopying, recording, or by any information retrieval system without written permission in writing by the author.

Published by Innovative Libraries, 2016.

195 Wakefield Road, Lepton, Huddersfield. HD1 3DH

andywalsh@innovativelibraries.org.uk

http://innovativelibraries.org.uk/

Although every precaution has been taken in the preparation of this book, the publisher and author assume no responsibility for errors or omissions. Neither is any liability assumed for damages resulting from the use of information contained herein.

Table of Contents

Introduction 1

Making partnerships work: practical strategies for building successful collaborations 13

Plotting and planning: analysing the alignment of learning support practices 31

Connecting with focus 57

Critical Collaboration: a narrative account of a newly established interprofessional team. 73

Terms of reference: working together to develop student citation practices 95

Transforming practice and promoting academic excellence through collaborative cross-unit partnerships 117

Living, learning, and the Library: A collaborative effort to bring information literacy, research, and beyond classroom experiences to residence halls 137

A tale of three cities: an interprofessional, inter-institutional collaboration 153

Index 175

Editor Biographies

Michelle Schneider is a Learning Advisor at Leeds University Library, supporting taught students to develop their academic and information literacies. She is an Associate Fellow of the Higher Education Academy and has recently been awarded a developmental University Student Education Fellowship from the University of Leeds. Michelle has been involved on a national level with both learning development and information literacy: she is a member of the ALDinHE Professional Development Working Group, she co-judged the 2015 CREDO Reference Award and was Runner up Information Literacy Practitioner of the Year in 2013.

Helen Webster is the Head of the Writing Development Centre, a learning development team based in the Robinson Library, Newcastle University. She has previously worked as a Learning, Educational and Researcher developer in both Staff and Student Services contexts at Cambridge University, the University of East Anglia and Anglia Ruskin University. She is a Senior Fellow of the Higher Education Academy (HEA), and member of the ALDinHE Professional Development Working Group. In addition to her interest in academic literacies, she was a member of the project team developing ANCIL (a New Curriculum for Information Literacy) and has created online digital literacy programmes for staff and students in Higher Education on a national level.

Jade is an independent blended learning consultant specialising in instructional design and online course development. Prior to going solo she worked as a learning technologist in higher education libraries, most recently at the University of Manchester Library where she was involved in the development of the award-winning My Learning Essentials programme. She continues to work closely with colleagues in higher education sector, and remains active in the library world through her work with the CoPILOT committee and on the CILIP Information Literacy Groups website editorial team. In 2014, Jade was runner up in the Association of Learning Technology (ALT) Learning Technologist of the Year award.

Introduction

This book is itself a product of an interprofessional collaboration. The three editors each have different professional backgrounds but we all work or have worked in learning support roles in higher education. Much of our respective careers have been shaped by interprofessional collaborative working, albeit not always consciously. This book has given us the opportunity to reflect on how this type of working has enhanced our knowledge, our practice, and the quality of the work and services we deliver in our day-to-day jobs. In light of this, we would like to open this book by sharing our personal experiences of collaborative working.

Michelle Schneider

My professional career began in academic libraries as an Information Literacy Officer. Teaching and learning has always been a significant part of my role. However, in retrospect, my first foray into teaching was what I would now consider to be "training" - helping students to navigate their way through databases to find academic information, or to format their references accurately. My entire approach to teaching was transformed when the previously centralised Skills Centre was brought into the Library and our two teams were integrated. My first project was to work with a small team of subject librarians and learning developers (LD) to create new teaching materials to tackle plagiarism. The LD helped us move away from a rules, regulations and referencing approach to a far more holistic view in which we explored the whole academic process that can lead to plagiarism, such as poor note making and understanding of academic writing conventions. My focus shifted from trying to help students to find definite answers or giving them a set of rules to follow, to empowering them to develop their own learning strategies and broader academic skills in order to help improve the way they learn and tackle their individual assessments.

For me, this experience highlighted the overlap between the two professions, and how much they complemented each other to such an extent that working in silos makes little sense. Since then, I have continued to embrace interprofessional collaborations, including working with e-learning professionals to design online learning experiences; with Careers Advisors on projects such as a recent digital literacy module; and with learning support professionals from other institutions (see chapter 8).

Jade Kelsall

Many of the most positive working experiences I've had have been collaborative. As a learning technologist working in academic libraries, I was often positioned at the intersection between overlapping professions. In my experience, cross-unit projects that bring together collective expertise from different professionals including librarians, learning developers and careers advisors are often a successful way of creating holistic learning experiences, and it is when these projects are truly collaborative in conception and design that the best results are created. Such cross-pollination of perspectives filters into my practice beyond individual projects. Working, talking and sharing with colleagues and friends who teach students is often a source of inspiration for ideas I can use within my online learning development.

As an instructional designer, collaboration is at the heart of what I do, and since making the move to independent contracting, every project is a new collaboration. My experiences working in such cross-professional teams have informed my approach to instructional design as a freelancer, particularly in understanding the value of bringing in a variety of perspectives and engaging project partners in the instructional design process from the outset.

Dr. Helen Webster

My own interest in interprofessional collaboration stems likewise from my career development. Following a period of academic subject teaching, I have worked in three closely related professions supporting learning and teaching in higher education: learning development (student facing), educational development (staff facing) and researcher development (supporting PhD and postdocs). In many ways, I viewed these as flipsides of the same coin. Yet in other ways, these are equally quite different professions whose distinct outlooks are shaped by their varying origins and the different professional backgrounds from which they have historically tended to recruit, there being no traditional qualification or training for any of them. I have become very interested in the way that the diverse professional backgrounds of those who work in each of these three roles has shaped and enhanced their conception of what it is they do and how to do it: academic, FE tutor, EAP tutor, counsellor, SPLD adviser, education researcher, management consultancy trainer. This has led me to reflect on how any one practitioner's self-conception and expertise can be enhanced with a more fluid, 'magpie-like' approach to professional expertise and identity. In practice, my own understanding of learning development as a culturally situated set of practices closely related to identity (Lea and Street 1998) and my one-to-one work with students has led to the realisation that to support students effectively is to develop a holistic approach. No one practitioner can be all things to a student, no matter how diverse their professional background, and I have sought out opportunities to collaborate with other services to improve my understanding of what they do, to enhance referral, and to create provision that brings together varied expertise to address complex issues. Working alongside colleagues with equally fluid professional backgrounds and those with more traditionally established professional identities, such as academics and librarians, has led to an interest in how these identities intersect, interact and develop.

A challenge arising from developing such an interprofessional approach to my own expertise has been that of integrating very different professional outlooks that can exist in tension with one another, no matter how they might agree on common goals. Two such areas are time management and stress management: vital to successful learning but invisible to and not mentioned in assessment criteria. Some years ago I initiated a project with a counsellor to develop a set of resources and workshops on procrastination and on exam and revision technique. I learned a great deal about effective collaboration from this partnership. It was true that we both shared a common goal in supporting students to manage their time and stress more effectively and to improve their chances of success, but I had not realised that different professions might not necessarily perceive that goal in the same way, nor how best to achieve it. Two very different outlooks were thrown into stark relief as my attempts as a trained teacher to begin by defining learning outcomes were met with bewilderment from my non-directive, client-led colleague! While the practicalities of a collaboration are of course important, this incident taught me how important it can be to engage also with more theoretical issues, and began my fascination with both interprofessional collaboration and professional development.

Why is this book needed?

There is surprisingly little in the literature about interprofessional collaboration between learning support professionals working in HE. Moreover, there do not seem to be any formal policies or frameworks within higher education in the UK to promote collaborative working across learning support services. This is in stark contrast to professions such as health, in which multi-professional teams and interprofessional working are strongly advocated from the point of student education through to everyday working practices. For example, the World Health Organisation (WHO) has developed a Framework for Action on Interprofessional Education & Collaborative Practice (WHO, 2010). This framework recognises that "collaborative practice strengthens health systems and improves health outcomes" (p.7) and sees "interprofessional collaboration in education and practice as an innovative strategy that will play an important role in mitigating the global health workforce crisis" (p.7).

A literature search for interprofessional and multi-professional working in the health profession reveals an abundance of research that has been undertaken to explore how interprofessional collaboration works in practice in a variety of health fields.

If interprofessional collaboration is promoted to improve outcomes in the healthcare profession, can we apply the same principles to learning support? Interprofessional collaboration between learning support professionals provides the opportunity to offer a more holistic service for students, which could lead to improved outcomes in their learning.

Who is this book for?

This book is aimed at learning support professionals including librarians, learning developers, and learning technologists, working in higher education.

The chapters are written by and for new professionals, established practitioners and managers of teams and services.

How to read this book

Interprofessional collaboration can take many different forms. Each of the chapters in this book reveals the diversity of contexts in which collaborative working occurs, as well as the different reasons for the development of such an approach. There is no one formula for making collaborations work. By bringing together the experiences and reflections from practitioners and researchers, this book highlights some guiding principles that can make collaborative working successful.

This book is not a linear narrative; it does not need to be read cover to cover. It is hoped that by sharing a number of different perspectives, case studies and examples of interprofessional collaborative working, you can delve into the chapters that are most relevant to your own context to draw out the principles that will work for you.

World Health Organisation, 2010. *Framework for action on interprofessional education and collaborative practice.* [Online]. [Accessed 03 October 2015]. Available from: http://www.who.int/hrh/resources/framework_action/en/

Chapter abstracts

Making partnerships work: practical strategies for building successful collaborations.

Sarah Parkes, Dr Julie Blackwell Young and Dr Elizabeth Cleaver

This chapter emphasises the key role of interprofessional collaboration in developing a distinct and appealing student experience, recognising that students are more likely to engage with the professional and social service provision that will have a significant impact on their student experience if it is integrated within the academic sphere.

Exploring first the advantages and challenges of partnership working and identifying five principles which characterise successful collaboration, it offers seven themes with practical actions that are central to effective collaboration. These approaches begin with the early stages of connecting aims through sound evidence base, identifying stakeholders and collaborators and their roles and responsibilities, through to sustaining partnerships through communication, measuring effectiveness and responding to change.

While there is a long-standing body of literature about collaborative, interprofessional working in other sectors such as healthcare, there is very little that relates to higher education. This research, drawing on a project to develop a 'toolkit' for use in universities, offers a practical and evidence-based foundation on which to build better partnerships.

Plotting and planning: analysing the alignment of learning support practices

Janette Myers

Myers offers a tool that can help to structure discussions around any collaborative initiative between professions, whether project-based, routine service provision or at the level of policy development. She describes how professions might use EN-MAP to clarify their own values and priorities, and the assumptions in which they are rooted, as well as those of collaborators.

Any provision for students makes assumptions about the level of autonomy that students are presumed to have or to attain as a graduate skill, and about the level of need (whether that be student need or institutional). The EN-MAP matrix offers a way to plot service provision against student autonomy and need to help unpick the different aims and assumptions that underlie any common collaborative service provision, to make visible differences in priority and goal, and to identify the impact of one profession's approach on the delivery of another.

As a case study, she examines an initiative to support retention and engagement for students who are not engaging with teaching by proactively contacting them about class absences or issuing automated reminders about coursework deadlines. In this instance, a discussion using EN-MAP highlighted how an administrative priority, assuming high need and low autonomy for either a specific group of students or a whole cohort, risked undermining colleagues' fostering of self-reliance as a graduate skill.

Connecting with focus

Barbara Dexter, Rita Kapadia and Ann Mullard

Dexter's account demonstrates how leadership that focuses on the transformation of working relationships rather than a transactional pursuit of outcomes can foster a working environment in which genuine exploration of collaborative potential can result from a restructuring and co-location of a number of different services and professions institutionally, physically and in terms of message to students.

A values-driven approach based on "servant leadership", and Corey's four leadership roles (role model, pathfinding, alignment and empowerment) together with the values that define the institution's distinct working culture are illustrated in four vignettes that show how productive, collaborative practice arose in areas that were formerly siloed in different departments. These areas were newly transformed as common goals were explored, provision was joined up and students benefitted from a seamless, coherent and enhanced service.

Critical Collaboration: a narrative account of a newly established interprofessional team.

By the UCA Canterbury Learning and Enhancement and Support Team (Lead author John Sutter)

Restructuring can be a disruptive and demoralising process, but Sutter et al show how it can present opportunities for more effective interprofessional team building and co-working. They demonstrate how an institutional and physical co-location of diverse student services and library teams as 'Learning Enhancement and Support', together with new roles expanded beyond traditional remits and practices, has resulted in a more collaborative approach and transformation of provision both within the new interprofessional team and beyond.

In seven 'lessons', they describe how an initial, positive openness among the new colleagues boosted morale and enabled better understanding of each other's roles and their own expanded practice. Overcoming previous siloed and 'territorial' approaches to really take advantage of the shared space and conversations that it enabled led to a more joined up provision, both in terms of referral and casework but also a shared vision and ethos. Exploring the theoretical underpinning of each other's practice has brought about a common shift from remedial, generic provision to one that is embedded and contextualised in the curriculum, and even challenges the curriculum and university assessment policy to embrace inclusivity.

Terms of reference: working together to develop student citation practices
Kim Shahabudin and Helen Hathaway

Following a physical relocation and structural integration of the Study Advice team into the Library at the University of Reading, this chapter discusses a collaborative project undertaken by members of this newly integrated service to tackle student issues around referencing.

The authors use this project as a case study to examine the benefits and challenges of collaborations, particularly between librarians and learning developers. While recognising that in many ways these two professions make ideal collaborators, the chapter analyses the potential challenges inherent in their integration including the different philosophies underpinning the professions.

The case study is situated within the wider context of the authors' experiences of the services' integration, and their reflections on how the two can continue to successfully collaborate to offer a better alignment of services for students and staff.

Transforming practice and promoting academic excellence through collaborative cross-unit partnerships
Vicki Bourbous and Tina Bavaro

This chapter illustrates how an interprofessional collaborative project was used as a catalyst to implement a transformative change in professional practice for liaison librarians at Australia Catholic University.

The authors outline a library-led project that aimed to develop the information and academic literacies of first year students by creating an online resource that brought together the fragmented support and advice offered by a number of services across multiple campuses. The project team included liaison librarians, academic skills advisors, an academic developer and an educational technologist.

This cross-unit approach was essential to ensure that the broad range of professional skills and expertise required to create such a resource were represented in the project team, and the authors present Design-Based Research as a framework for supporting such collaborative projects.

Equally, it was only through working with partners from other professional backgrounds that the librarians were able to challenge their perceptions of information literacy and how it could be taught. Having structured professional development activities and interventions built into the project gave the librarians the opportunity to reflect upon the nature of their role, resulting in a long-term transformation of their practice.

Living, learning, and the Library: A collaborative effort to bring information literacy, research, and beyond classroom experiences to residence halls

Ngoc-Yen Tran and Elizabeth Cantor

This chapter explores an unusual collaborative partnership between the university library and accommodation services at the University of Oregon. Both services identified a common goal: to enhance student engagement. Librarians needed to reach students beyond the classroom in those courses where information literacy was not embedded in teaching, and Residence Life coordinators needed to integrate campus accommodation further with the academic community to capitalise fully on the social and graduate skills development benefits of living on campus. An initiative to include a full library service within a new residence building offered new possibilities, but a close, mutually respectful and ongoing dialogue was essential to ensuring that these were realised and sustained.

Underlying their account is an analysis of the drivers behind each phase of the collaboration.

Any student-facing initiative in higher education would of course claim student learning as its aim and there is evidence that this leads to more successful collaborative partnerships. However, external accountability, top-down directives and the distinctive ethos of the institution itself may also play a significant part in shaping any collaborative effort, imparting different emphases or directions that will colour or exist in tension with the goal of enhancing student learning. An awareness of the dominant driver behind each phase of their collaboration and a jointly reflective approach to reframing and taking ownership of their shared goal to ensure the primacy of student learning helped two quite disparate services create a successful and productive service.

A tale of three cities: an interprofessional, inter-institutional collaboration

Michelle Schneider and Jade Kelsall

This chapter offers a different perspective on collaborative working. It examines a project that was not only interprofessional but also inter-institutional, and instigated by the practitioners themselves.

The Student Guide to Social Media was created by a small team of learning support professionals from the Universities of Leeds, Manchester and York. The project lead chose to go beyond institutional boundaries to choose her co-collaborators, and selected people that she knew would bring the skills and expertise required for the project.

In this chapter, the authors discuss the lessons learned from this project. They share their reflections on the experience, highlighting what they did successfully and what they would have done differently with the benefit of hindsight.

Offering practical advice throughout, this chapter aims to help other professionals to instigate and successfully implement their own informal collaborative projects.

Making partnerships work: practical strategies for building successful collaborations.

By Sarah Parkes, Dr Julie Blackwell Young and Dr Elizabeth Cleaver

About the authors

Sarah Parkes

Tutor for Transition and Retention, Newman University, Birmingham

In partnership with a range of colleagues, Sarah explores and develops in-curricula and co-curricula strategies for improving student transition and retention on undergraduate programmes at Newman. Her principal interests include notions of institutional transformation within programme design and structural organisation that develops staff capacity to enable student success, rather than looking for increased homogeneity within the student body. Sarah is Project Leader of the HEA & Paul Hamlyn "What Works: Student Retention and Success Change Programme" at Newman, Fellow of the Higher Education Academy, Programme Leader for HEADstart, and teaches on the BA(hons) English Literature & BA(hons) Youth and Community Work programmes.

Dr. Julie Blackwell Young,

Academic Quality Manager, Abertay University, Dundee

Dr Julie Blackwell Young works in Teaching and Learning Enhancement and her current role involves working with both professional and academic staff as well as senior staff to advise on quality assurance issues whilst maintaining a quality enhancement focus. Prior to working in the quality arena, Julie was a Chartered Psychologist and senior lecturer in psychology specialising in forensic psychology and reproductive psychology.

Julie's interests lie in student engagement with curricula and university processes, quality enhancement, professional/academic identities and technology enhanced learning. Julie is a Senior Fellow of the Higher Education Academy and teaches on the Postgraduate Certificate in Higher Education Teaching.

Dr Elizabeth Cleaver

Director of Learning Enhancement and Academic Practice. University of Hull

In her current role, Elizabeth provides leadership, management and strategic oversight of Quality Assurance and Enhancement, Teaching Development, Technology Enhanced Learning and Public Engagement for Learning and Teaching, working across the University of Hull and engaging with colleagues from a range of academic and professional service teams. Her interest in partnership working arose from her move to work in central university services after having spent her early career as a faculty-based academic. Elizabeth is Chair of the Heads of Educational Development Group (UK) and a Principal Fellow of the HEA.

Introduction

Collaborative working between the social, professional and academic areas is now recognised to be of key importance for student engagement, retention and success (Thomas, 2012a; Quinlan, 2011). In a sector now characterised by high levels of uncertainty and change, staff from a range of disciplines and areas within higher education institutions (HEIs) are increasingly required to work together in partnership with their students to create a cohesive, holistic student experience which ultimately retains, engages and enables success (MacFarlane, 2011; Quinlan, 2011; Thomas, 2012b).

However, it is interesting to note that while literature on cross-organisational partnership working in sectors such as health and social care, local government and education is both evident and plentiful

(Alexander et al., 2001; Perkins et al., 2012), there is, in contrast, less literature exploring partnership working within the higher education sector (both intra and inter-institutional).

This chapter draws on research exploring how academic and professional staff work together to enhance the student experience, outlining seven key themes for effective partnership-level work within higher education.

The student experience: what is it?

Over the last decade the United Kingdom (UK) higher education sector has experienced a number of far-reaching changes which have impacted on student recruitment and institutional funding. Indeed, the vision delivered in the Government's 2010 White Paper "Students at the Heart of the System" reconceptualised the cost of university as one that the student should fund, rather than something to be supported by the state and the student together (Great Britain, 2011).

Changing the funding model in this way has led many commentators to predict that students will develop a more consumerist mind-set, expecting more from a university experience that costs the student money. This expectation has subsequently been fed by the absence of any real differential between fees as most institutions have chosen to charge students near to or the maximum of £9,000 per annum (Patton, 2011; Sedghi & Shepherd, 2011) and recent Competition and Markets Authority (CMA) guidance for students around their consumer rights (CMA, 2015). Thus, with the overall cost of a higher education similar across the UK for those students that pay, HEIs have had to distinguish themselves in other ways. Developing and investing in the academic, support and social dimensions of the student experience has been one way in which institutions have endeavoured to achieve this (Bulpitt, 2012).

The very concept of 'the student experience' is not easily defined. In spite of its increasing appearance in university strategic documents, the idea of the student experience has remained contested: in an increasingly diverse higher education sector, each student is now recognised to have their own 'experience' based on the context in which it is viewed or defined (Jones, 2008). As Parkes et al. (2014a) acknowledge, any one student's 'experience' can be influenced by the level of their involvement in and engagement with a range of HEI academic, social and support areas, alongside a range of other environments with which students are likely to come into contact by virtue of studying at a particular institution. Such areas and environments can include but are not limited to:

- student support areas such as study skills, welfare or disability
- information technology and/or elearning departments
- libraries and other learning resources, both physical and virtual
- accommodation and catering services
- academic service departments such as registry, quality or exams and assessment
- students' unions including support services, social events and networks.

Moreover, there are many aspects of each individual student's experiences including life-wide factors such as home life, employment and past educational experiences that are simply not within an institution's control or influence.

The complexity of this concept notwithstanding, this chapter takes the definition of the student experience provided by Thomas and May's (2011) "Student Engagement to Improve Student Retention and Success" model (see also Thomas, 2012a: 18): viz. the successful generation of a sense of belonging within students that goes on to affect their experience of Higher Education.

Why work collaboratively?

In her report What Works: student retention and success programme (2012a), Liz Thomas investigated a programme of activities aimed at improving the student experience and aiding retention and progression across 22 UK HEIs. Similar to the findings of Quinlan (2011), Thomas views the academic sphere as central to the experience and success of students. In short, when both the professional support and the social domains - interactions with services and student development activities - are introduced and delivered through the academic sphere, students are more likely to access and engage with them.

To enable this to happen, partnerships and collaboration across institutional boundaries and silos needs to take place. Such partnerships can be powerful (Powell and Glendinning as cited in Perkins et al., 2010) as they can afford outcomes gained through sharing innovation (Duke, 2003), utilising others' expertise (Whitchurch, 2013) and/or increasing efficiency, that are greater than any one partner could produce on their own. By bringing together groups from across an HEI, there is therefore potential to unite previously fragmented aspects of student support work that can result in the enhancement and promotion of a holistic student experience (Bulpitt, 2012). Moreover, students will see an integrated institution where different aspects of provision complement one another, creating a whole educational experience (Doskatsch, 2003; Quinlan, 2011). Such an experience can foster a sense of belonging in students which in turn increases engagement in study and with the institution, thus increasing the likelihood of completing their qualification successfully.

There is, of course, a further potential advantage that emanates from such collaborative working. Macfarlane (2011) notes that when a greater understanding of others' roles, skills and attributes is developed through working with new people in new ways, good working relationships can be established between areas that might have been perceived as non-cognate. Thus, through offering staff opportunities to expand their skills and experiences, both staff and institution benefit (Bulpitt, 2012). Bulpit further argues that within the new fees structure where students may perceive themselves as consumers of a higher education experience, this can only lead to positive outcomes.

Alongside the varied benefits of partnership working come some challenges to staff members' identities and roles. Whitchurch (2008a; 2008b; 2012; 2013), who conceptualises the site of partnership work as a 'third space' rather than being located in either academic or professional space, identifies that partnerships forming across different working areas can lead to inequitable working models. This is further supported by Macfarlane (2011) who argues that divisions of labour may result between academic, support and professional service staff; academics may feel disempowered and de-skilled as aspects of their academic roles are taken away from them by up-skilled specialist support staff or 'para-academics'. Conversely, specialist support staff may feel as if they are seen as interlopers and are not really valued for their skills and abilities (Whitchurch, 2013). As Parkes et al. (2014a, p.8) discuss, this is a key factor to consider when building effective partnerships between academic and professional services staff. If professional staff or indeed students themselves, via mentoring or peer assisted learning schemes, begin to take on what might be perceived to be aspects of academic roles, the reactions that accompany this may be counterproductive both to the partnership itself and to wider institutional strategic developments.

Whitchurch also asserts that her conceptual 'third space' is often an organic environment (2008a; 2008b) where activities do not always take place within the traditional hierarchies and networks of the institution. This potentially produces issues of accountability, resulting in the need for clear rules of engagement, responsibilities (to the project and others) with clear project or ownership by a senior member of staff (see Levitt et al., 2011) within an HEI.

Towards a self-assessment toolkit for collaborative working

This section of the chapter takes as its starting point the findings of a study undertaken by the chapter's authors that explored how partnerships between academic and professional staff work, and what factors in particular impact on the ability of such partnership projects or activities to improve the subsequent experiences of students. We hope that the findings of this research and its associated toolkit will be useful to institutions who wish either to consider their readiness for, or to improve their previous experiences of, partnership working.

The terms 'collaboration' & 'partnership' are used interchangeably due to their frequent synonymous usage, though we acknowledge there are subtle differences between the terms (sMcKimm et al., 2008). For the purposes of the chapter, these terms can be understood as professional and academic staff working together to engage in activities within a higher education institutional setting.

To develop our understanding of partnership working, the research sought to answer the following questions:

1. Who is currently developing or has already developed successful partnership models for delivering and enhancing the student experience?

2. What is the experience of those who are developing or have already developed these partnership models?

a. How have these models been constructed or evolved?

b. What staffing structures and arrangements have been needed to implement these models?

c. What changes to organisational structures have been required and how have these been implemented?

d. How have students been involved in shaping these models?

e. How have leadership, management and governance helped or hindered these developments?

f. What is the staff experience of working within these models and how has this fed into the model?

3. How can these experiences be used to support future initiatives in this area?

The research was conducted by means of questionnaires sent to HEIs and further education colleges engaged in HE work throughout the UK; focus group interviews across ten UK institutions; and a post-data collection validation workshop with representatives from nine UK institutions. Full details of the research methodology can be found in Parkes et al., (2014a; 2014b).

The five key principles of partnership working in higher education

The research enabled the identification of five key principles which underpin effective partnership working. These are suitable for a variety of contexts, and they provide a foundation on which institutions can build practical solutions to take collaborations forward.

Principle 1: Understand motivations for developing the partnership, and the extent to which they may go on to help or hinder the development and sustainability of collaborations.

Principle 2: Recognise that strategic support is necessary if partnerships are to be successful and sustainable to affect institutional change.

Principle 3: Ensure suitable reward and/or recognition systems are in place for staff and students involved in partnership activities.

Principle 4: Recognise the organic nature of change and prepare those involved for feelings of messiness, uncertainty and anxiety.

Principle 5: Develop a culture of honesty, openness and disclosure to underpin the workings of each partnership.

Other pre-requisites for success

For collaborations between staff groups and students to be effective, it is crucial that the project or initiative is wholly appropriate for a partnership approach and must have consensus from all involved. This agreement should include consideration of the following issues (links to the key principles are included in brackets after each pre-requisite):

- securing an executive sponsor, which indicates support of the partnership at the strategic level (Principle 2)
- compiling a detailed and clear focus for the collaboration that recognises the input of and impact on all stakeholders (Principle 1)
- ensuring a clarity of vision and terminology, which can help to develop a culture of communication, honesty and openness (Principle 5). Negotiated, often new, shared understandings and

meanings can enhance the ability of the group to work together (Parkes et al., 2014a)
- identifying the resources that will be needed and action to be taken before the partnership is initiated. This may include suitable reward and/or recognition systems (Principle 3) and is likely to be an indicator of strategic support (Principle 2).

Seven themes for operational success

Following the analysis of focus group data and the post-data collection validation workshop discussions, we were able to identify some of the practical considerations necessary for partnership success and to categorise them into seven themes.

While none of the seven themes is new in partnership work per se, together, and within the context of contemporary higher education, they provide a strong framework through which institutions can actively make improvements to the student experience through partnership working.

1. Using contextual evidence to connect aims and goals.

As with all change work undertaken in higher education, the aims and goals of the collaboration must identify and utilise a relevant evidence base that underpins and contextualises the purpose and direction of the partnership. This will also assist with supporting and meeting the internal and external motivations of those involved.

Where possible, the evidence should resonate with overarching departmental and institutional strategies; partnership outcomes and outputs should demonstrate how strategic objectives will be met or supported. This is of vital importance to ensure the partnership is supported by those responsible for the strategic direction of the institution.

Such evidence could be drawn from relevant internal and/or external baseline data such as previous institutional and/or sector-wide projects, experiences and evaluations.

Equally, evidence can be taken from measures like Higher Education Statistics Agency statistics, National Student Survey scores, departmental or subject satisfaction surveys, module evaluations, module completion rates or re-sit rates, for example.

2. Engaging stakeholders

This was highlighted as vital to a project's success across our research sample, and included varied opportunities for staff and students to learn about, engage with, contribute to and receive feedback on the project or partnership. Such engagement provides opportunities for partnerships to learn from feedback (both positive and negative) from those directly involved in the project, as well as from those affected by the project. Activities designed to achieve this must be accessible for all staff and can include the production of physical or digital newsletters, launch events with networking opportunities, all staff/student briefings alongside dedicated web space with project blogs and/or videos to develop understanding and engagement in the partnership. If partnerships sit outside the usual institutional structures, care needs to be taken when deciding how communication between the team and other stakeholders is achieved (Whitchurch, 2008b). Such care is required to mitigate for inadvertently creating feelings of disempowerment in academic quarters or a perceived under-valuing of skills and abilities of professional support staff (Macfarlane, 2011; Whitchurch, 2013).

3. Identifying contributors

Whilst engaging stakeholders is important, of equal significance is identifying the right people to deliver the outputs and outcomes of the partnership. For many, the involvement of staff and students will be due to their professional role, institutional level of responsibility and/or personal interest. However, proactive recruitment of individuals with innovative strategies for engagement or whose knowledge and skills are helpful to the partnership can be important for success. As such, any opportunities for involvement from interested staff and students should be communicated from the outset alongside any rewards associated with involvement.

Contributors could be identified formally through internal institutional-level advertisements such as newsletters, emails, or committee discussion; at the departmental level via meetings or professional development events or located at the individual level in conversation with line managers. Informally, if individuals have been identified because of their innovative method, they could be approached by leading members of the partnership to ascertain their level of interest and potential commitment to the endeavour.

4. Defining roles and responsibilities

In order for partnerships to be effective, staff and students need the various roles and responsibilities within the project or initiative clearly defined from the outset. Furthermore, these need to be communicated to all stakeholders within and external to the collaboration to ensure that expectations of individuals and roles are realistic.

There should be regular reporting mechanisms to a committee or formal reporting/steering group that will ensure that the entrusted activities can meet the aims and objectives/terms of reference of the partnership/project. Roles and responsibilities can be articulated through group terms of reference, with levels of responsibility and reporting clearly defined and agreed within the team from the beginning. This should include discussion of, and agreement on, projected time-commitments and/or the workload balances of the individuals involved. Returning to Principle 3, above, ensuring that workload balance is considered can be a form of recognition for the staff involved in partnership work. Through utilising formal reporting structures (see Principle 2), the ability to influence, make decisions and enact change across the institution within the scope of the partnership/project can become real.

The role of leadership and management within partnerships is often paramount to their success. Leadership within partnership working is necessarily multi-dimensional; creating and supporting inter-personal relationships, building trust and understanding complexity are some of the key skills and values needed (Williams, 2002; 2010).

As partnership working necessarily involves spanning formal and informal institutional boundaries, it requires leaders who value and understand the need to do this. Such leaders are identified through their ability to find new and innovative solutions, to engender high levels of trust, to engage well with and to appreciate the positions and perceptions of others (Williams, 2002).

5. Communication and dissemination

An integral part of all seven themes for successful partnership working is construction of a clear and inclusive communication and dissemination strategy. This should detail mechanisms for the institution-wide dissemination of news and updates to all staff and students and include an action plan that generates institution-wide understanding of key stages, times and outputs from the partnership project or initiative.

However, before external communication takes place, of particular importance is the identification of the key ways that effective and regular communication will take place between those involved in the partnership: formal reporting; sharing practice(s) and team-building exercises. Providing regular departmental, institutional and sectorial dissemination of activities associated with the partnership is key and could employ of a range of communication technologies - such as virtual learning environments, project wikis, blogs and social media - to engage a range of interested parties in discussion about the partnership/project as it progresses. Principles 4 and 5 are of key importance here as effective communication can be a useful tool in mitigating wider concerns and anxieties whilst the project is in any messy and uncertain phase.

6. Evaluating/measuring effectiveness

With the increasing pressure on efficiency, having effective methods of measuring success must be built into the partnership/project from its inception. Projects may use existing institutional evaluation mechanisms or may involve the creation of something new, involving all members of the partnership/project group in establishing evaluation processes with clear deadlines for completion and reporting.

The selected evaluation techniques must be underpinned by empirical evidence and/or philosophical/conceptual approaches that utilise a range of measures that will appraise and triangulate effectiveness. Such techniques will necessarily be context specific and must be flexible enough to embrace the analysis of emerging or unexpected outcomes. The ability to evaluate and use evidence to change direction as necessary can be key to ensuring continuing strategic level support of a partnership (Principle 2).

7. Sustainability and change

Increased expectations of efficiency often come in tandem with pressures to justify resource level and staffing. Thus, any partnership project or initiative must ensure that its resource is flexible enough that it can respond to any changes (including funding reductions) within HE. Improving flexibility therefore requires periodic review of the aims and objectives or terms of reference in the light of evaluation activities and departmental, institutional and sectorial environmental changes (Principle 1).

Reviews should include an evaluation of membership, roles and responsibilities. These should be adapted and changed where necessary, and in consultation with those involved.

For short term or finite partnerships/projects, a clear exit strategy with recommendations for embedding practice within 'business as usual' needs to be clearly developed from the outset as part of the project brief.

Concluding comments

This chapter has outlined some of the key principles and activities that have been shown to lead to operational success for those working on projects across academic and professional services boundaries with the purpose of improving the student experience. These findings emerged from research undertaken with individuals across a range of UK HEIs who have been directly involved in partnership projects aimed at improving the student experience.

Acknowledging the growing importance of cross-institutional and inter-departmental work in the area of the students experience within HEIs, this chapter has discussed the research findings underpinning the 'Self-Assessment Toolkit' (Parkes et al., 2014b) which has been developed to support all types of collaborative work within HE and includes suggestions for activities to be undertaken before, during and after the partnership work to ensure success.

The toolkit has been developed to help those wishing to build effective partnerships in practice. It aims to support HEIs in their reflection on how their operational procedures, services and teaching practices, when coupled with their physical and virtual environments, can be developed to promote a sense of belonging that enables students to make the most of their experience of higher education. Making partnerships work is key to the success of these developments. If the environments, procedures, services and teaching that students encounter during their studies are not perceived by students as isolated aspects of university life, but connected parts of their 'student experience', they cannot and should not be developed in isolation from one another.

To access the 'Self-assessment Toolkit' please visit:
https://www.heacademy.ac.uk/sites/default/files/resources/prof_service_partnerships_instituuse_blank_toolkit_final_200214_update.pdf

References

Aldrich, H. 1999. *Organizations evolving.* London: Sage

Alexander, J.A., Comfort, M.E., Weiner, B.J. and Bogue, R. 2001. Leadership in collaborative community health partnerships. *Nonprofit Management & Leadership.* 12(2), pp.159-175.

Bell, J. 2005. *Doing your research project.* Maidenhead: Open University Press

Bolden, R., Gosling, J., O'Brien, A., Peters, K. and Haslam, A. 2012. *Academic leadership: changing conceptions, identities and experiences in UK higher education.* London: Leadership Foundation for Higher Education.

Bulpitt, G. 2012. Leading the student experience: Super-convergence of organisation, structure and business processes. London: Leadership Foundation for Higher Education.

Competition and Markets Authority. 2015. *Higher education. Undergraduate students: your rights under consumer law.* [Online] [Accessed 8 November 2009]. Available from: https://www.gov.uk/government/uploads/system/uploads/attachment_data/file/415732/Undergraduate_students_-_your_rights_under_consumer_law.pdf

David, M., Parry, G., Vignoles, A., Hayward, G., Williams, J., Crozier, G., Hockings, C. and Fuller, A. 2008. *Widening participation in higher education: A Commentary by the Teaching and Learning Research Programme.* London: Teaching and Learning Research Programme and Economic and Social Research Council.

Doskatsch, I. 2003. Perceptions and perplexities of the faculty-librarian partnership: an Australian perspective. *Reference Services Review.* 31(2), pp.111–121.

Duke, C. 2003. Changing identity in an ambiguous environment: A work in progress report. *Higher Education Management and Policy.* 15(3), pp.51-67.

Fullan, M. 2007. Leading in a culture of change: Personal action guide and work book. San Francisco: Jossey Bass.

Gill, R. 2006. Theory and practice of leadership. London: Sage

James, C. 1999. Institutional transformation and education management. In: Bush, T., Bell, L., Bolam, R., Glatter, R. and Ribbins, P. eds. *Educational management: Redefining theory, policy and practice.* London: Sage, pp.142-154.

Jones, R. 2008. *Student retention and success: a synthesis of research.* [Online]. Higher Education Academy. [Accessed 8 November 2009]. Available from: http://www.heacademy.ac.uk/resources/detail/inclusion/wprs/WPRS_retention_synthesis

Laws, S., Harper, C. and Marcus, R. 2003. *Research for development.* London: Sage

Levitt, R., Goreham, H. and Diepeveen, S. 2011. *Higher education collaborations: Implications for leadership, management and governance.* [Online]. London: Leadership Foundation for Higher Education. [Accessed 10 June 2013]. Available from: http://www.lfhe.ac.uk/en/components/publication.cfm/S3%20-%2001

Lukes, S. 1974. *Power: a radical view.* Basingstoke: Macmillan.

Macfarlane, B. 2011. 'The morphing of academic practice: Unbundling and the rise of the para-academic.' *Higher Education Quarterly.* 65(1), pp.59-73.

McKimm, J., Millard, L. and Held, S. 2008. Leadership, education and partnership: Project LEAP — developing regional educational leadership capacity in Higher Education and health services through collaborative leadership and partnership working. *The International Journal of Leadership in Public Services.* 4(4), pp.24–38.

Quinlan, K. 2011. *Developing the whole student: leading higher education initiatives that integrate mind and heart.* [Online]. London: Leadership Foundation for Higher Education. [Accessed 19 June 2013]. Available from: http://www.lfhe.ac.uk/en/components/publication.cfm/ST%20-%2001

Parkes, S., Blackwell Young, J., Cleaver, E. and Archibald, K. 2014a. *Academics and professional services in partnership literature review and overview of results.* [Online]. Higher Education Academy. [Accessed 8 June 2014]. Available from: https://www.heacademy.ac.uk/sites/default/files/prof_service_partnerships_report_final_200214_updated_1.pdf

Parkes, S., Blackwell Young, J., Cleaver, E. and Archibald, K. 2014b. *Academics and professional services in partnership summary report and self-assessment toolkit.* [Online]. Higher Education Academy. [Accessed 8 June 2014]. Available from:

https://www.heacademy.ac.uk/sites/default/files/resources/prof_service_partnerships_instituuse_blank_toolkit_final_200214_update.pdf

Patton, G. 2011. Universities to charge average £8,600 tuition fees. *The Telegraph.* [Online]. 28 March. [Accessed 17 February 2013]. Available from:
http://www.telegraph.co.uk/education/universityeducation/8411357/Universities-to-charge-average-8600-tuition-fees.html

Perkins, M., Bauld, L. and Langley, D. 2010. Learning from the partnership literature: Implications for UK University/National Health Service relationships and for research administrators supporting applied health research. *Journal of Research Administration.* XLI(1), pp.49-59.

Sedghi, A. and Shepherd, J. 2011. Tuition fees 2012: what are the universities charging? *The Guardian.* [Online], 23 June. [Accessed 17 February 2013].Available from:
http://www.guardian.co.uk/news/datablog/2011/mar/25/higher-education-universityfunding

Thomas, L. 2012a. Building student engagement and belonging in Higher Education at a time of change: final report from the What Works? Student retention & success programme. London: Paul Hamlyn Foundation/HEFCE

Thomas, L. 2012b. Building student engagement and belonging in Higher Education at a time of change: a summary of findings and recommendations from the What Works? Student Retention & Success programme. Paul Hamlyn Foundation

Thomas, L. and May, H. 2011. Student engagement to improve retention and success model. In: Thomas, L and Jamieson-Ball, C. ds. *Engaging students to improve student retention and success in higher education in Wales.* [Online] HEA, p.11. [Accessed 23 March 2012].Available from:

http://www.heacademy.ac.uk/assets/documents/inclusion/retention/EngagingStudentsToImproveRetention_final_English.pdf

Watson, L. 2008. It's not about us: It's about them. In: Weaver, M. ed. *Transformative learning support models in Higher Education: educating the whole student*. London: Facet Publishing

Williams, P. 2002. 'The competent boundary spanner'. *Public Administration*. 80(1), pp.103-124.

Williams, P. 2010. Special agents: The nature and role of boundary spanners. *ESRC Research Seminar Series. Collaborative Futures: New Insights from Intra and Inter-Sectoral Collaboration*. University Of Birmingham, February 2010.

Whitchurch, C. 2008a. Shifting identities and blurring boundaries: The emergence of Third Space professionals in UK Higher Education. *Higher Education Quarterly*. 62(4), pp.377-396.

Whitchurch, C. 2008b. Professional managers in UK Higher Education: Preparing for complex futures. Final Report. London: Leadership Foundation for Higher Education.

Whitchurch, C. 2012. Expanding the parameters of academia. *Higher Education*. 64, pp.99–117.

Whitchurch, C. 2013. Reconstructing identities in higher education: The rise of third space professionals. London: SRHE.

Yorke, M. and Thomas, L. 2003. Improving the Retention of Students from Lower Socio-economic Groups. *Journal of Higher Education Policy and Management*. 25(1), pp.63-74.

Plotting and planning: analysing the alignment of learning support practices

By Janette Myers

About the author

Dr Janette Myers

Senior Lecturer in Student Learning and Support, St George's, University of London

Having taught in further, adult and higher education, Janette moved into advice and guidance and student support in higher education before returning to learning development. Experience of these multiple roles has provided a particular set of perspectives on the rewards and challenges of interprofessional working. Wishing to understand why student support exists in its current forms, Janette carried out PhD research on the origins of student support activities and their influences on current policies and practices. Janette is an active member of the Association for Learning Development in Higher Education.

Introduction

The complex multiprofessional environment that has developed in modern higher education in relation to learning support and wider student support practices has led to the potential for many competing and complementary policies, procedures and activities to exist. Moving from multiprofessional to more collaborative interprofessional working requires employing methods to enable colleagues to be aware of each other's roles, professional practices and understandings. This chapter explores a method developed to enable both collaborative and individual thinking about practices and the intersections between them. EN-MAP is an ideal-type matrix, named for its function in enabling mapping, that permits practices to be analysed, mapped and hence evaluated.

Two critical experiences led to the research that underpins this chapter. I was in a hybrid role, working on an academic contract in student support with a remit to promote student engagement and retention. In a meeting on the development of students' academic practice, a colleague shared his views on students and their support. Students, he told us, were the worst prepared for higher education and the worst motivated he had ever seen. This had not been the case some time ago, and the types of support we were discussing in the meeting were spoon-feeding. Spoon-feeding was a bad thing (Myers, 2010). Simultaneously, my role involved telephoning students who had not been attending or engaging with the Virtual Learning Environment. I was surprised that in four years of doing this, no student ever asked why their behaviour was my business; indeed, many thanked me for contacting them.

Both of these experiences caused me to think. I wondered how learning how to learn in a new context could be taught and promoted to students and colleagues in a way that gave the message that this was a valuable developmental activity, linked to the creation of subject knowledge, rather than a remedial activity for the supposedly underprepared. In relation to attendance interventions, I became interested in ideas of autonomy and the ways autonomy was valued and developed in some projects, but not in others. These contradictions were most apparent when interprofessional or multiprofessional groups were working together or in tandem, but also occurred intraprofessionally. It became important to look at the range of professionals who were sending messages to students, both explicit and implicit, about their understandings of the role of the university and the place of the student within it. Researching the history of the development of student support practices helped me to understand the perspectives of different professional groups, and identified some overarching themes in our practice. Finally, I developed EN-MAP to enable us to examine these themes and messages.

This chapter will illustrate how EN-MAP can be used to analyse the diversity of provision and practice in student support and learning development, and to examine the interactions, tensions and contradictions between these diverse practices. Practitioners can use it to identify their positions in relation to specific practices and to each other.

I will use illustrative examples from the last 40 years, because it is important to identify the context for issues we experience today and to recognise the influences that the past has on current practices.

Background and context

Many factors have been involved in producing the current diverse picture of support practices. Recognising the role of these complex and interacting factors enables us to locate our practices, and those of others, in their historical and policy context. There are many national and local factors that have led to colleagues from a wide range of professional backgrounds and experience collaborating to support students. This diversification has resulted in an increased number of roles and backgrounds as people work in what Celia Whitchurch (2008) has termed the 'third space', a professional area that exists both across and outside more traditional boundaries in higher education. Many of the roles that can broadly be considered third space are aligned to student support, including learning development and engagement, student advice and student services, and information skills and literacy.

I can trace my own career in higher education to two policy events. One was the shift to modularised degrees that led to a recommendation for the creation of a 'para-academic service' to provide educational guidance and academic support (HEQC, 1994, p.276). The other was the emphasis placed on the development of generic skills in the Dearing Report (NCIHE, 1997), which led to an increase in the numbers of Learning Centres intended to facilitate this development (Gosling, 2001); many of those working in learning development and/or information literacy will owe their roles to initiatives that followed Dearing. Michael Shattock has helpfully characterised the higher education policy environment as either internally generated "inside-out" or externally generated, "outside-in" (Shattock, 2006). This is useful to our understanding of student support because our practices have developed as a result of a set of interactions between these influences, creating diverse practices and rationales between and within professions. If we were starting from scratch we might act differently, but we are not, and awareness of this can help our practice. Individual interests and different professional histories have created inside-out factors and various government policies and wider social change created the outside-in, and both these sets of influences interact. For example, learning developers working with a social justice framework in which they seek to empower students from disadvantaged groups were able to use funding derived from government policy that rewarded higher education institutions for retaining students. These factors and the interactions between and within them have resulted in a rich heterogeneity of practice that can be argued to reflect either a diverse student and institutional landscape or a fragmented approach with the potential for negative outcomes - or quite possibly both.

Examining the development of student support over time shows that ideas of the development of autonomy by students, often manifested as independence, are one important theme. Another is varying perceptions of the level and content of student need. Both historical and current practices of student support indicate that these are key concerns, right up to the recent QAA Quality Code in which students' needs are discussed and the term 'independent learner' is used, see for example Chapter B3 *Learning and Teaching* (QAA, 2012) and Chapter B4 *Enabling Student Development and Achievement* (QAA, 2013).

One effect of the diversity of provision and fragmentation of responsibility is to produce multiple approaches that may not align. This can send mixed messages to students. Thus, although the development of autonomy is one of the primary goals of higher education, its development is often contradicted by practices which are based on assumptions about students' needs for care, protection or control (Myers, 2013).

Attendance and engagement practices are a good example of this. Outside-in drivers prioritise the importance of attendance over the development of autonomy, inside-out social justice approaches prioritise development and hence autonomy, but both perceive a high need for support.

Unpacking the policy drivers, current and historic, alongside perceptions of need and autonomy facilitate collaborative working and educational outcomes. For example, engagement may be encouraged through the use of text message reminders to students. This removes the need for students to actively seek and use information provided and so, it could be argued, reduces the opportunity for them to take responsibility for their own time and information management. Examining an example of such a project, a multiprofessional collaboration of administrative, academic related and academic colleagues to promote retention, shows that its outcomes were complex (Harley et al., 2006). Text messages were successful in reminding students of deadlines, so had a positive effect on engagement, and students reported high level of satisfaction with receiving deadline reminders by text. However, I would argue that the language of satisfaction also shows a less positive effect on the development of autonomy.

"I don't know what everyone else is like but I am terrible at checking my email and some people are terrible at checking [the VLE] for any information like that so to get these texts to your phone, because we have always got our phones on us...."

"Well it has let me know pretty quick and obviously there is a deadline, it has to got to be done by next week. But it is good, it has got me doing it, I came in and did it"

(Harley et al., 2006, p.37)

Students are expressing rather negative views of their own abilities to manage their time and motivation. This would appear to be at odds with the wider project's stated aim of enabling students to develop as independent learners, although the project does emphasise that the process is developmental (Cook, 2006). It is argued that this provision is of benefit during the transition period at the beginning of higher education, to intervene in what one student described to me as a 'long dark tunnel' from enrolment to first assessment. This argument also implies a need to explore whether there should be a managed transition to more independence.

Plotting and planning on EN-MAP would enable those designing and implementing provision to explore, acknowledge and maybe resolve conflicting ideas about long term development of autonomy and short term support of high need.

The EN-MAP Matrix

EN-MAP is an ideal type matrix that enables educational activity to be plotted against the two concepts of perceived autonomy and student need that form the axes. This makes the relationship of activities to ideas of autonomy and need more explicit, providing a concrete way of discussing these themes and enabling practices to be compared. It should be noted that perception is in the eye of whoever is using the matrix, and the discussion that arises from those different perceptions is an important part of the plotting process. There are no 'right' answers or 'correct' locations. One benefit of the process is to permit different professional groups to work together to recognise each other's perspectives and take a holistic view of their various policies and practices.

EN-MAP

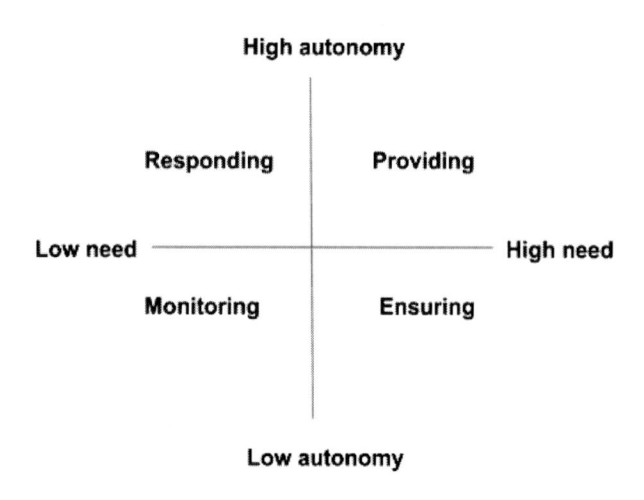

High autonomy

Responding	Providing

Low need ———————————————— **High need**

Monitoring	Ensuring

Low autonomy

The quadrants

Each quadrant is characterised by particular interactions of ideas of autonomy and need that underpin types of provision. Analysis and discussion is more important than finding a 'correct' placement; provision may or may not sit neatly in a single location. I will explain each quadrant, and give some examples of how provision might be located, then I will explain how the matrix can be used in collaborative working.

The *Responding* quadrant

High autonomy

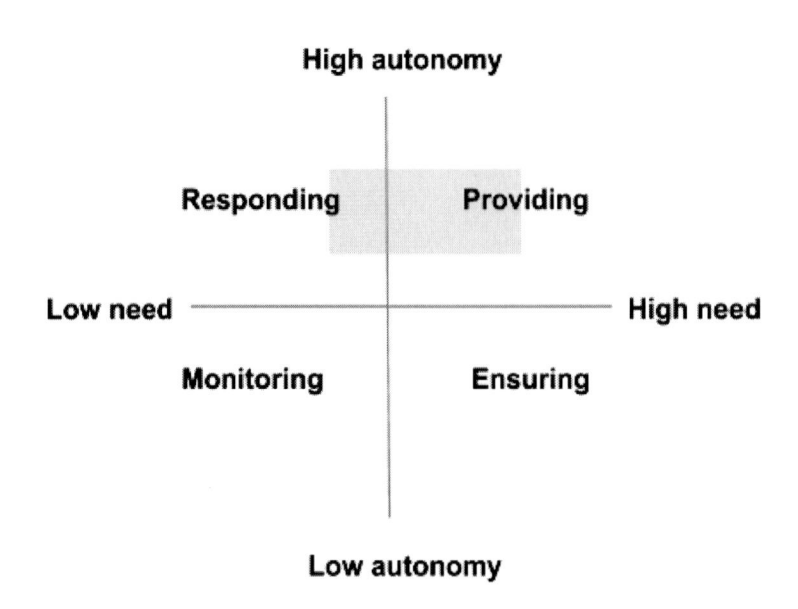

Responding	Providing
Monitoring	Ensuring

Low need — **High need**

Low autonomy

Provision that is based on implicit or explicit assumptions of high autonomy and low need is located in the *Responding* quadrant. When used implicitly, *Responding* forms of support are provided reactively as need arises, often based on assumptions that few students have those needs.

An example would be traditional forms of personal tutoring in which students are given a personal tutor with the expectation that they will only access their tutor if in difficulty. The implicit assumption is that personal tutoring is for responding to problems and few students have problems, therefore minimal resource is allocated. This type of model is discussed in a review of transition for non-traditional students (UCAS, 2002).

When explicitly employed and proactively used, *Responding* forms of support draw on ideas of adult learning, and of students' competence and ability to decide whether to access support. An example would be centralised extra-curricular study skills support that is based entirely on student self-referral. This model can mean that academic and learning development teams are working in parallel rather than interprofessionally. They may have similar attitudes to autonomy, in that students are able to choose to access the service, but different approaches to need, with contrasting remedial and developmental approaches. Also, some commentators working with other perceptions of student need have identified this type of reactive model as making unfounded assumptions that students will recognise their support needs and know how to seek the means to address them, see for example Thomas (2006) in relation to reactive models of personal tutoring.

A key feature of this quadrant is that the assumption of low need means it is anticipated that few students will access support; resourcing can then become a problem if demand is larger than expected. Plotting and planning via EN-MAP enables these conflicts to be explored and examined.

The *Monitoring* quadrant

High autonomy

Responding	Providing
Monitoring	**Ensuring**

Low need ──────────────── High need

Low autonomy

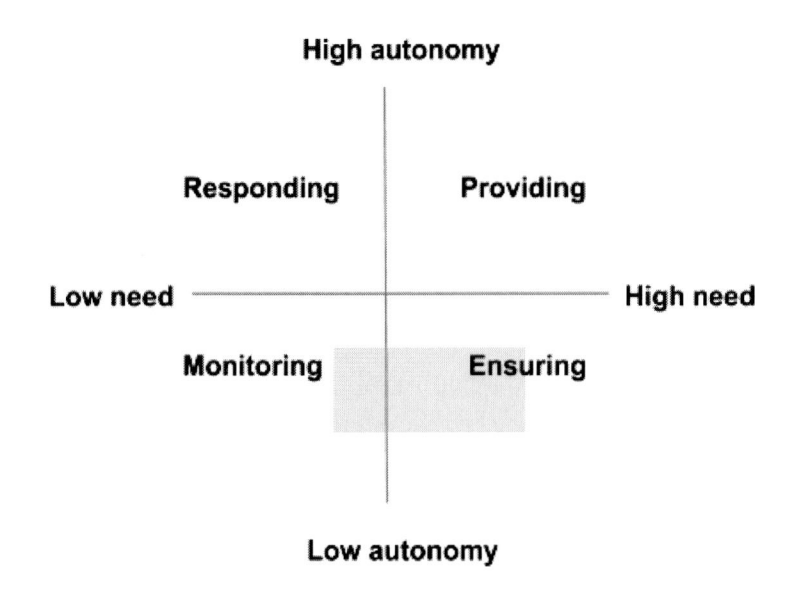

Located in the *Monitoring* quadrant, low need and low autonomy provision is rarer now than it was in the past. When monitoring is used now, it is usually in the context of high rather than low need, although later discussion of attendance monitoring will analyse these assumptions and show how an interprofessional team used EN-MAP to explore and analyse them. Low need practices include the type of close supervision that occurred for reasons which were more to do with custom and practice, or with a goal of controlling students, than with perception of high need in students. This would include the type of control that was common in traditional residential accommodation, in which students' movements were restricted via curfews (Silver and Silver, 1997).

Although unusual, more recent examples can be found. Studies in the US have argued that medical students who have a record of low-level unprofessional behaviour, such as poor initiative, diminished capacity for self-improvement and irresponsibility, are over-represented among those doctors who subsequently undergo disciplinary action for more severe misconduct in their medical careers (Papadakis et al., 2005). This has led to recommendations for the teaching and monitoring of professionalism in the medical curriculum for all students. Identification of unprofessional behaviour leads to 'remedial' programmes and further monitoring. Despite low incidence, and therefore low need in most students, the high significance of misconduct and the lack of other predictive factors are used to justify monitoring all students. As a learning developer I discuss what students have learned from this this process with my medical education colleagues. Does it develop professionalism or the ability to spot which absences and misdemeanours attract penalties?

Diminished autonomy in these models is related to potential consequences of transgressive behaviour and to institutional needs located outside individual students, rather than to strong constructions of student need. Plotting and planning via EN-MAP would enable a fuller range of assumptions and implications, such as the potential effects on the development of autonomy, to be explored.

The *Ensuring* quadrant

High autonomy

Responding | Providing

Low need —————————————— High need

Monitoring | Ensuring

Low autonomy

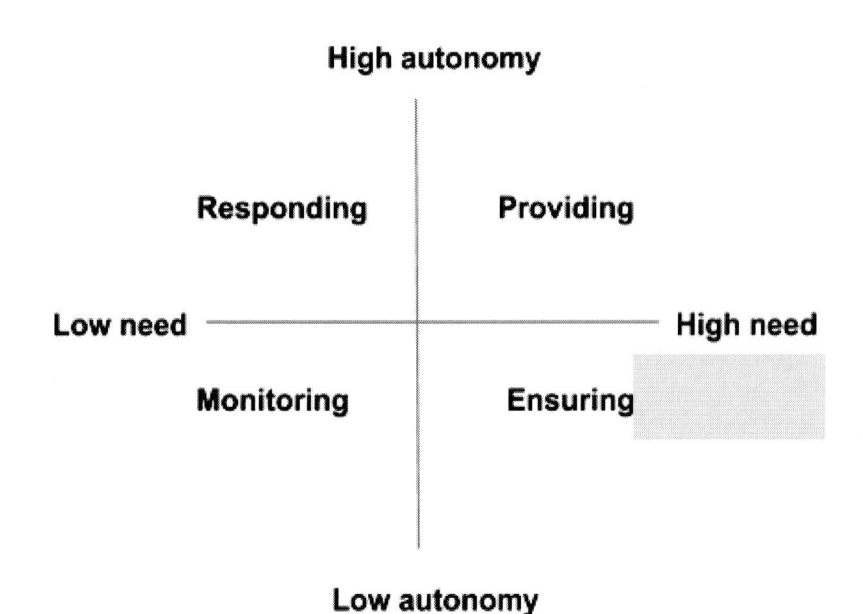

Low autonomy and high need forms of support are located in the *Ensuring* quadrant. In such support activities, students are seen as in need of support because they are vulnerable to academic failure and other harms. When support is ensured, students are afforded little personal control over accessing support, and may be protected from the consequences of their (in)actions. The text message reminder activity discussed earlier could be located here (Harley, 2006).

Increased provision in this quadrant has stemmed from some very different drivers, illustrating the significance of both inside-out and outside-in influences on higher education (Shattock, 2006). Outside-in influences include the various stages of expansion of participation in higher education and the more recent move to outcomes-based funding for recruitment and retention.

An early example of the interaction between internal and external drivers can be seen in the expansion of participation in higher education that took place during the 1950s.

One internal approach to the perceived need to socialise these unfamiliar students into the ways of the university was to strongly advocate the acculturating effects of living in university halls of residence (University Grants Committee, 1957). Later social justice approaches to inequality, applied to current widening participation strategies, have identified certain groups as having different access to the social and cultural capital that promotes engagement and achievement, and so these groups have been identified for particular forms of support, sometimes compulsory, for example when supporting under-represented groups on high status courses (Garlick and Brown, 2008).

Another shift over time has been from targeted to inclusive models for support. The idea that specific groups can be identified for targeted support has been questioned, and a more integrated and inclusive approach in which support is provided for all has been advocated (Thomas, 2012). Embedded learning development is a good example of integrated, inclusive approaches that often draw on collaborative work between learning developer, student support, academic and administrative colleagues, sometimes reflecting priorities set at senior management level, see for example the work championed by the University of Huddersfield (ALDinHE/University of Huddersfield no date). If students have little or no choice over whether to participate in this provision, then it could be located in the *Ensuring* quadrant because autonomy is low, whilst need is high. This will be more fully discussed later in the chapter, showing how plotting and planning enables these decisions to be analysed and understood.

The *Providing* quadrant

High autonomy

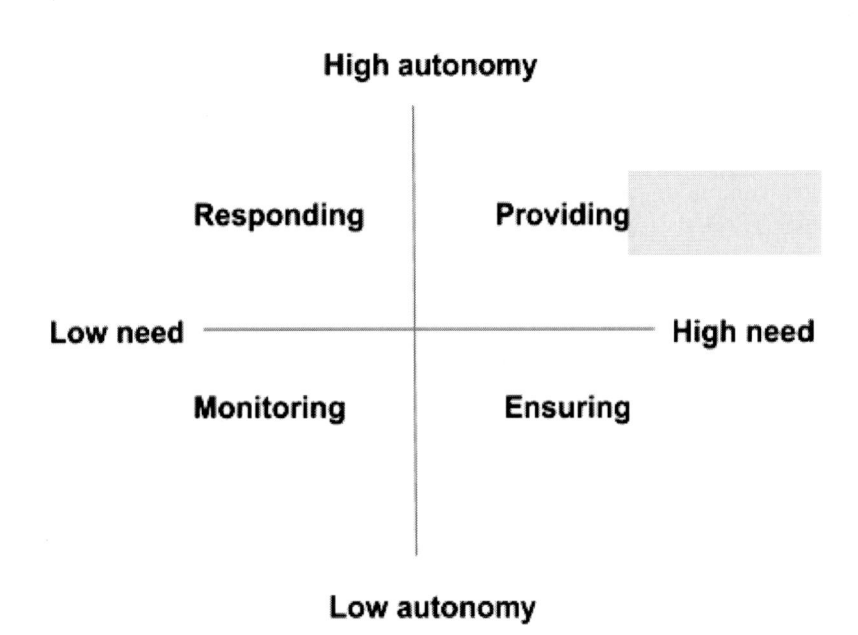

Responding | **Providing**

Low need ──────────────── **High need**

Monitoring | **Ensuring**

Low autonomy

Student support in which the student is perceived to have a high degree of both need and autonomy is located in the *Providing* quadrant. An example of this can be seen at Oxford Polytechnic, which designed its modular degree based on the principle that student responsibility and choice would be an underpinning feature of the scheme and that students have a high need for information in order to exercise this responsibility (Watson, 1989). Providing the means to develop and exercise autonomy is seen as part of the educational process and hence as part of the remit of many professional groups within higher education. The view that drop-out rates could be reduced by the provision of adequate information to support informed choice is an example of this model, as poor course choice has been identified by students as a reason for dropping out (Yorke, 1999).

Students are assumed to make rational choices about course and institution based on evaluation of information, and therefore to have a high need for information and the ability to exercise the autonomy to access it. The current policy of providing students with standardised Key Information Sets about higher education providers derives from this approach (Higher Education Funding Council England, 2013).

High autonomy models stem from a belief that students do not require protection, even if this leads to negative outcomes such as higher dropout rates for students with non-traditional entry routes (Robinson, 1968).

In his thought-provoking and prescient book, Earwaker (1992) argues that challenge is an important part of an educational experience. It may make students feel uncomfortable or unsafe, but, undergoing and managing this is part of the educational experience. It is useful to look at high autonomy views and models of support for a different perspective, as they tend to come from periods when student satisfaction and retention were not on the agenda. Currently we can see examples of acceptance of Earwaker's view that support should be located with the course, as the primary source of student identity, rather than in centralised services. For example, Larkin and Richardson (2013) argue that student need is created by a highly challenging educational environment and that this should be recognised in the curriculum, making it the appropriate arena for learning development.

Using EN-MAP to plot and plan can enable institutions to decide whether they should take educationally justifiable risks, and to include students in the decision and the dissemination processes.

Using EN-MAP

EN-MAP allows policy and practice to be analysed by distinguishing key features, plotting, and comparing different types of provision. I have used the matrix as a tool for talking and thinking when working in direct collaboration with others, and as a tool for thinking when working alone, although outcomes usually lead to collaborative solutions. Examples of both uses will be provided.

Who can use EN-MAP?

The short answer is that anyone can use EN-MAP. The longer answer is that I have used it in a number of contexts centred around student support activities, ranging from the academic to the administrative ends of the spectrum. The next section gives an extended example of its use within a student services team. I have also used it to enable learning developers and academics to examine their provision when integrating subject matter and academic practices development; with mixed groups of student support/services and administrative teams when considering how their processes contribute to the development of a learning environment; and with uni-professional groups evaluating the impact of their policies, both intended and unintended.

Tool for talking and thinking

EN-MAP can provide a structure for talking and thinking when bringing colleagues from different areas together. Recent work on academic and professional services partnerships emphasises the need for this interaction (Parkes et al., 2014).

A large student administration and services team in an Australian university used EN-MAP at a whole department staff development day to launch a review of practices. The full range of professional and student services were present at the event, seated in interprofessional groups. There was an initial presentation and discussion of the matrix axes and the educational role of professional services, then groups worked on large copies of EN-MAP to position some of their key practices on the matrix. Two questions emerged that could be applied to analyse the practices: 'how educational is this practice?' and 'what would happen if we stopped doing this?'. One of the practices discussed was sending frequent emails to students to remind them to register onto their modules. They decided that this practice was placing administrative convenience over educational principles, sending the message that students did not have to take responsibility for noting and responding to deadlines.

Discussion of perceptions of need identified several types of need. One was for students to register their modules so they could continue to study; not registering in time could result in loss of choice or even of progression. Another high need was for students to learn to manage time and requirements so that deadlines were met. The team felt that these two needs were potentially in conflict if the solution was to send repeated reminders. Finally they noted their own need from an administrative perspective: if large numbers of students do not register their modules, managing a modular scheme is very difficult. Interestingly, using EN-MAP resulted in all those present identifying primarily as educators. They located the previous reminder practice in the *Ensuring* quadrant and decided that this was unintentional on their part, potentially reducing autonomy and the opportunity to learn to be independent and self-managed. The outcome was to move to the *Providing* quadrant; they would reduce reminders to students to register modules, and communication would now be couched in terms of the importance of co-operation between staff and students to manage a modular system. Consequently they provided clear information, reduced reminders and made plans to deal with any difficulties caused by lower or later levels of module registration.

This type of activity promotes challenge and discussion of established and proposed practices. The specific nature of the EN-MAP task provides a focus for teams to discuss and question received wisdom and their assumptions. When working collaboratively, these activities can get everyone on same page - or at least give everyone sight of all the pages, permitting the book to be organised. They also provide clear evidence that quality assurance and review is taking place in a meaningful way. Chapter B4 of the Quality Assurance Agency [QAA] Quality Code on *Enabling Student Development and Achievement* has indicators which suggest that universities should "define, coordinate, monitor and evaluate roles and responsibilities for enabling student development and achievement both internally and in cooperation with other organisations" (QAA, 2013, p.7). An activity such as this is a good source of evidence to show that the wide range of people who enable student development are working together to keep this area under review.

Tool for thinking

As discussed in the introduction, the two areas of practice that began my investigation of this topic were student attendance monitoring and models for the provision of learning development. I will now explain how developing and using EN-MAP has enabled me to think about these areas. I could not claim to have come to definite conclusions about how to proceed in all circumstances, but I have developed ways of evaluating options and models, and communicating that evaluation.

The complex question of whether attendance should be compelled, and therefore monitored, is a good example of the distinction between the high need/low autonomy *Ensuring* and the high need/high autonomy *Providing* quadrants. There is a tension between affording students the right to decide when and how to create their own learning opportunities and deal with the consequences of their actions, and seeking to maximise student success and make effective use of teaching resources. Macfarlane (2012) argues that attendance monitoring practices form part of a surveillance culture that values presenteeism over intellectual engagement, and creates conditions of reduced autonomy whilst using a rhetoric of the development of autonomy. It is a literal manifestation of control, requiring students to register their presence. Compulsory attendance and voluntary attendance represent opposite ends of the autonomy axis; a monitoring process in which students are encouraged to review their choices represents a point in between.

When reviewing attendance monitoring it is important to be aware of the context, located in the complex relationship between inside-out and outside-in factors. Outside-in factors began with changes in funding methods: institutions had to retain students in order to earn their income. This was reinforced by other cultural and regulatory changes. School and college students have become accustomed to monitoring with the use of registration systems that trigger automatic alerts to school administration and parents. Students who received 16-19 Bursaries or Educational Maintenance Allowance were accustomed to monitoring because receipt of these is dependent on attendance.

Within higher education, the need to meet UK Visas and Immigration Tier 4 sponsor licence obligations has created a more accepting climate for attendance monitoring.

Inside-out factors were located in student-centred approaches to widening participation. Models related to feelings of belonging (Tinto, 1987) or to ideas derived from Bourdieu about possession of social or cultural capital, such as knowledge of how universities work and provide support (Thomas, 2002), were applied to issues such as retention and attainment of students from under-represented groups.

There is a complex relationship between internal and external contextual drivers, and both have led to similar conclusions based on ideas that non-attendance puts students at risk of drop out, therefore attendance should be monitored and non-attendance addressed. Thus support could be targeted at those in most need because they are high risk of dropping out. This was and is often couched in terms of student benefit rather than disciplinary language.

Projects to prevent drop out are likely to involve multiprofessional groups, both in planning and implementing projects and strategies, and this is often advocated as a key to success (Johnston, 2002). The following example looks at the way a collaborative team was created and came to understand and develop its practice through the use of EN-MAP. I began by compiling a list of reasons for the importance of attendance; some of the factors noted were as follows. Attendance is important:

- to the individual student, because of the educational risks of non-attendance
- to the educational environment, because some learning activities cannot take place unless students are there and contributing, therefore not attending disrupts other students and staff members

- to the institution, because non-attendance has important effects on the successful management of the university, which, in turn affects students.

This implies high need and so provision is placed at that end of the Need axis, although I was also aware that the institutional need could be argued not to directly impact on students. In my practice at the time, I worked with students to mitigate the consequences of their non-attendance so they could get back on track, and this involved contact with colleagues on an ad hoc basis.

I decided that this approach could afford students little autonomy over their learning and engagement and so this provision would be in the *Ensuring* quadrant. Following this reflection I felt that there was a risk that the ultimate learning for the student was that someone else would sort things out for them, preventing rather than enabling student development. Also, as I worked with more students, I realised that there were systematic institutional issues that were acting as a barrier to their engagement, so I began to adjust the way I practised to try to avoid the unintended consequences. I took responsibility for institutional barriers to engagement and facilitated students to address individual barriers themselves. As a result my team increased our collaborative and interprofessional work. A staff development programme for academics enabled colleagues to gain a better understanding of students' learning experiences before coming to university, and therefore understand the nature of the academic transition students were expected to make. There were also simple but significant organisational issues. Many students had problems accessing the timetable via the VLE at the beginning of term or finding the right room in the maze of corridors and one missed class often turned into several. Therefore a number of teams including IT, facilities management and student administration worked to improve this and attendance improved. Some of the need to adapt lay with the organisation rather than within the student, calling into question the rationale for attendance monitoring. EN-MAP enabled collaborative working across a number of areas to enhance students' ability to attend and learn from classes without using attendance monitoring practices that reduced autonomy.

Thinking about this again while writing this chapter, I wondered whether sometimes it might be most appropriate to acknowledge that external imperatives mean that some types of attendance monitoring are restricting autonomy without being directed at student need, placing provision in the Controlling quadrant. They exist for reasons that are not always educational, or to do with the best interests of individual students.

One approach would be for all concerned to decide together whether avoiding the language of support entirely and explaining the reasons for these practices to students would mean that we can engage with them in a more open and honest way.

Drawing on ideas developed through plotting attendance monitoring, I started to think about the move to embed learning development in the curriculum and student support in the course, evidenced and advocated in work such as Earwaker (1992), Wingate (2006) and Thomas (2012). Whilst developing the matrix I struggled with whether embedded learning development could be located in the *Providing* or *Ensuring* quadrants. I hypothesised that the embedding model was operating at the high need end of the axis, but rejected a simple idea of unpreparedness or unfamiliarity that needed to be remedied. The idea of situated approaches to learning that need to be developed in their unique disciplinary, higher education context that underpins embedded models was helpful (Wingate, 2006). At first I located this embedded approach at the low autonomy end of the Autonomy axis because students have no choice about whether to access provision if it is co-taught with their subject matter, unless they choose not to attend. A combination of high need/low autonomy would place this model somewhere in the *Ensuring* quadrant. When questioning this, it was helpful to consider the meaning and context of autonomy. It seems reasonable to begin with an assumption that students will participate in their chosen course of study. If developing the ability to learn is seen as integral to developing subject knowledge, then choosing to study includes choosing to learn how to study. Students are then no more compelled to learn to study than they are compelled to study subject matter. Once I had linked learning development to knowledge creation I moved the embedded model to the *Providing* quadrant.

Creating a context in which everyone needs to learn about how to study in order to understand how knowledge is created in their discipline removes the idea of high need as a deficit and re-presents it as an integral part of learning in a discipline. The high-challenge environment creates the need, rather than a deficit in the student (Earwaker, 1992, Larkin and Richardson, 2013).

This process created more contexts for collaboration. Plotting with EN-MAP meant I was able to explain and advocate the approach to course teams including managers, the academics who were teaching and the administrators who were managing the course. We created teaching materials and supporting staff development based on learning how research draws on and refines previous work, providing a context for the development of the ability to plan, sequence and structure an argument and for understanding the need for citation and referencing.

Conclusion

The richness and potential of a diverse higher education environment needs to be examined if it is to be experienced and communicated as coherent, and this requires collaborative working. Plotting and planning using EN-MAP permits colleagues to use this specific task as an aid to discussing their respective approaches to learning and student support. The EN-MAP axes are derived from research into models of student support in higher education and enable two important concepts underpinning much support provision to be explored and interrogated. This provides a method for interprofessional communication and analysis which has the added benefit that it contributes to quality review and enhancement.

References

ALDinHE/University of Huddersfield. [no date]. *Integrating Learning Development*. [Online]. [Accessed 19 March 2015]. Available from: http://aldinhe-embeddingskills.hud.ac.uk/homepage

Cook, A. 2006. Gaining Independence Slowly. In: Cook, A., Rushton, B.S. and Macintosh, K.A. eds. *Supporting students: extended induction*. Coleraine: University Of Ulster, pp.7-11.

Earwaker, J. 1992. *Helping and supporting students*. Buckingham: Society for Research into Higher Education and Open University Press.

Garlick, P.B. and Brown, G. 2008. Widening participation in medicine. *British Medical Journal*, **336**, pp.1111-1113.

Gosling, D. 2001. Educational development units in the UK- what are they doing five years on? *The International Journal for Academic Development*, **6**(1), pp.74-90.

Harley, D., Winn, S., Pemberton, S. and Wilcox, P. 2006. Student Messenger: the Role of SMS text messaging in supporting student transition to university. In: Cook, A., Rushton, B.S. and Macintosh, K.A. eds. *Supporting students: extended induction*. Coleraine: University Of Ulster, pp.29-42.

Higher Education Quality Council [HEQC]. 1994. Choosing to change: extending access, choice and mobility in higher education. London: HEQC.

Higher Education Funding Council England. 2013. *Unistats and key information sets*. [Online]. [Accessed 6 August 2014]. Available from: http://www.hefce.ac.uk/whatwedo/lt/publicinfo/kis

Johnston, V. 2002. *Improving student retention – by accident or by design?* [Online]. [Accessed 19 March 2015]. Available from: http://www.exchange.ac.uk/issue1.asp

Larkin, H. and Richardson, B. 2013. Creating high challenge/high support academic environments through constructive alignment: student outcomes. *Teaching in Higher Education.* **18**(2), pp.192-204.

Macfarlane, B. 2013. The surveillance of learning: A critical analysis of university attendance policies. *Higher Education Quarterly* 67(4), pp.358–373.

Myers, J. 2010. Why support students? Continuity and change in forms of student support in English higher education. PhD thesis, University of London.

Myers, J. 2013. Why support students? Using the past to understand the present. *Higher Education Research and Development.* **43**(4), pp.509-602.

National Committee of Inquiry into Higher Education [NCIHE]. 1997. *Higher education in the learning society. Main report* [Dearing Report]. London: NCIHE.

Parkes, S., Blackwell Young, J., Cleaver E. and Archibald, K. 2014. *Academics and professional services in partnership. Summary report and self-assessment toolkit.* [Online]. [Accessed 7 August 2014]. Available from: https://www.heacademy.ac.uk/sites/default/files/resources/Prof_Service_Partnerships_toolkit_final_201214_updated.pdf

Papadakis, M.A., Teherani, A., Banach, M.A., Knettler, T.R., Rattner, S.L., Stern, D.T., Veloski, J.J., and Hodgson, C.S. 2005. Disciplinary action by medical boards and prior behavior in medical school. *New England Journal of Medicine.* **353**, pp.2673-2682

Quality Assurance Agency. 2012. *UK Quality Code for Higher Education - Chapter B3: Learning and teaching.* [Online] [Accessed 6 August 2014] Available from: http://www.qaa.ac.uk/publications/information-and-guidance/publication?PubID=171#.U-IxyKMaBdg

Quality Assurance Agency. 2012. *UK Quality Code for Higher Education – Chapter B3:Learning and Teaching.* [Online]. [Accessed 6 August 2014]. Available from: http://www.qaa.ac.uk/publications/information-and-guidance/uk-quality-code-for-higher-education-chapter-b3-learning-and-teaching

Quality Assurance Agency. 2013. UK Quality Code for Higher Education - Chapter B4: Enabling student development and achievement. [Online]. [Accessed 6 August 2014]. Available from:

http://www.qaa.ac.uk/publications/information-and-guidance/publication?PubID=172#.U-IxC6MaBdg

Robinson, E. 1968. *The new polytechnics.* London: Cornmarket.

Shattock, M. 2006. Policy drivers in UK higher education in historical perspective: 'inside out' 'outside in' and the contribution of research. *Higher Education Quarterly,* **60**(2), pp.130-140.

Silver, H. and Silver, P. 1997. *Students: Changing roles, changing lives.* Buckingham: SRHE and Open University Press.

Thomas, L. 2002. Student retention in higher education: the role of institutional habitus. *Journal of Education Policy.***17**(4), pp.423-442.

Thomas, L. 2006. Widening participation and the increased need for personal tutoring. In: Thomas, L. and Hixenbaugh, P. eds. *Personal tutoring in Higher Education.* Stoke on Trent: Trentham Books Ltd, pp.21-32.

Thomas, L. 2012. Building student engagement and belonging in Higher Education at a time of change: final report from the What Works? Student Retention & Success programme. [Online]. [Accessed 6 August 2014]. Available from:http://www.phf.org.uk/page.asp?id=1715

Tinto, V. 1987. *Leaving college.* Chicago: University of Chicago Press.

UCAS. 2002. *Paving the way.* Cheltenham: UCAS

University Grants Committee. 1957. R*eport of the sub committee on halls of residence.* London: Stationery Office.

University of Huddersfield. [no date].Integrating learning development. [Online]. [Accessed 19 March 2015]. Available from: http://aldinhe-embeddingskills.hud.ac.uk/homepage

Watson, D. 1989. *Managing the modular course.* Milton Keynes: Society for Research into Higher Education.

Whitchurch, C. 2008. Shifting identities and blurring boundaries: The emergence of third space professionals in UK higher education. *Higher Education Quarterly,* **62**(4), pp.377-396.

Wingate, U. 2006. Doing away with 'study skills'. *Teaching in Higher Education.***11**(4), pp.457-469.

Yorke, M. 1999. Leaving early: undergraduate non-completion in higher education. London: Falmer.

Connecting with focus

By Barbara Dexter, Rita Kapadia and Ann Mullard

About the authors

Barbara is Professor of Academic Leadership and Director of Learning & Teaching at Buckinghamshire New University. She has national and international publications on management and educational development, careers and managing change.

Rita is a Career Development Consultant at the Careers and Employability service at Buckinghamshire New University. Her current work remit includes enabling students and recent graduates of the University to make effective career related decisions by developing their career management skills.

As Senior Lecturer in the Learning Development Unit at Bucks, **Ann** has extensive teaching, course leadership and management experience in universities and colleges. Independent consultancy in career development and jobseeker training underpins her enthusiasm for combining her mathematics and EAP expertise to support graduate employability skills.

Introduction

This chapter discusses how a values-driven approach can have a positive impact upon interprofessional collaboration. It is a reflective piece; a time for the lead author to take stock after a year in a new post as Director of Learning and Teaching at Buckinghamshire New University (Bucks). It also an opportunity to share how team members have been fostering joint and collaborative working, connecting with the focus on an improved service for students and staff.

The word 'service' is chosen with care and purpose, mainly as I bring to the role my stated preference for working within an ethos of "servant leadership" (Greenleaf, 1998) in an institution whose values are 'Clarity, Openness, Respect and Delivery on Commitments' (CORD). 'Service' does not mean in any way subservience, as we all have a clear and important role to play within the University and in the sector as a whole.

This chapter discusses the connecting values and principles that inform and guide our work. Some theoretical underpinning is given, since, in Lewin's famous words, "there is nothing so practical as a good theory" (1951, p169), but the chapter's main focus is on transferable practice for effective collaboration within interprofessional working. Several examples of cross-directorate and institutional working provide examples that could be adopted at other institutions of these ideas in practice.

Context

In 2012, Bucks restructured the Student Services Directorate, creating a new Learning & Teaching Directorate to include:

- Careers & Employability (C&E), providing one-to-one support, workshops and online guidance. In the restructure, a new suite of activities were introduced, including managing alumni and mentoring, a temps and volunteering agency, enterprise development and online developments alongside more traditional careers information, advice and guidance.
- The Learning Development Unit (LDU), a primarily student-facing service providing study skills and academic development to support student learning and success. This is mainly on an appointment basis, and ranges from pre-sessional through to PhD support. LDU also provides various tailored workshops and courses.
- Open 4 Learning (O4L), our technology-enhanced learning team, providing support and training for staff and students on our Virtual Learning Environment (VLE) and new initiatives. O4L is

a small department of three staff and their expertise is much in demand, particularly for web-based online content development.

In addition to these existing teams, we are building a new Directorate team for academic development to work on our Continuous Professional Development Framework (CPDF) to be accredited by the Higher Education Academy (HEA). This new team will encompass staff development, projects, pedagogic and institutional research, HR processes and excellence awards.

The Directorate's work is informed by our Learning & Teaching Strategy 2013-17, including goals of building the capacity of our staff and increasing provision that supports students' enterprise, employability and leadership. For the Directorate to be successful following its restructure, I had to ensure that I provided an appropriate leadership approach to foster sound interprofessional working.

Why a values-driven approach?

Much of institutional life, especially in medium and large corporations, be they in the private, public or even the not-for-profit sectors, is based around *'doing'* rather than *'being'*. Target-driven managerialism has a focus on actions and accountabilities; results and reporting; metrics and measurement. It avoids the human dimension and yet as individuals, we intuitively sense that this is the most important aspect of our work. When people assume the role of manager, they frequently employ transactional language, focus on the wrong things and in HE have diminished "the humanity of the institutions" (Hussey and Smith, 2010, p.26).

A values-driven approach, on the other hand, forces consideration of what is fundamentally important to the way we live *and* work. Most professions have explicit values that may complement each other, although this is not always the case. When different professionals are brought together after a significant change such as a restructure, it can provide fantastic opportunities for interprofessional working but can also cause conflict if such values are not aligned.

Therefore, an appropriate, clear and strong leadership style is required to help foster effective interprofessional working and collaboration.

A values-driven approach to leadership and management

Values-driven approaches are at the heart of leadership and management at Bucks. The institution's values of Clarity, Openness, Respect and Delivery on Commitments (CORD) are used in processes from recruitment and selection, through training and appraisal, to institutional policy-making. Targets and metrics cannot be overlooked, but they must have a clear purpose and align with these values in order to justify their introduction and usage.

My values and approach to leadership are informed by servant leadership as I believe that it is best both for individuals *and* for the organisation as a whole, and holds high relevance for collaborative working.

Larry Spears (2002, p.4) describes servant leadership as "a long-term, transformational approach to life and work". Based on the work of Robert Greenleaf (1998), it has ten key characteristics:

Listening	Conceptualisation
Empathy	Foresight
Healing	Stewardship
Awareness	Commitment to the growth of people
Persuasion	Building community

Covey (2002) talks about "four roles of leadership", which can be seen as modelling the characteristics identified above. The first is to be a role model through acting with integrity and credibility. The trust and openness that arise from known, shared and enacted values enable solid relationship-building for interprofessional working. Within my team of four managers for example, shared values include a preference for transformational rather than transactional approaches to our work and this provides the principles underlying our discussions.

While constantly aware of budget and resource constraints that mainly focus on the transactional nature of relationships with students, the transformational perspective underpins our main *raison d'être* and keeps the commitment to the growth of our students at the heart of what we do.

The second is what he calls "path-finding". Our path is provided by the Learning & Teaching Strategy but requires our shared vision of the best ways to implement it. This involves conceptualisation of the best ways of working together and the foresight that comes from knowing your people, fostering collaboration through knowing who will work best with whom. For that, I believe in 'seek first to understand', and so I spent a lot of time trying to get to know each member of the Directorate staff and their needs. I continue to have an open-door policy and try to practise 'managing by wandering about'. These sound leadership behaviours include listening, empathy and sometimes healing. They are practical skills that can be learnt and practised, and will promote a healthy working environment for collaboration.

Covey's third role of leadership is alignment, aligning vision and values with systems and structures. He reminds us that "you can get commitment and involvement by many people if your value system is truly exemplified by your organisation's structure and policies" (p29). The restructuring that I inherited helped in that I had not been the disruptive agent, but came in to build the new teams. As a newcomer, I was able to bring fresh eyes and ideas, questioning where I saw misalignment and working with my Pro-Vice Chancellor (PVC) to ensure that the disparate groups of professionals came together effectively within the new directorate.

The fourth leadership role espoused by Covey is empowerment, which resonates with the growth of our people and the building of community. By empowering Directorate staff and providing support and resources to ensure they can work effectively, work is accomplished whilst continuing to develop people. For example, one member of the Careers team wanted to extend her remit and be more involved in project work. I knew that an institutional initiative was in need of review and evaluation, so I persuaded the PVC to allow this person to undertake the review with my guidance. She was given one day per week off from her normal duties, and we also funded her to attend a project management course. The review meant that she had to work across both faculties and other departments, and thus helped to build relationships.

It was a significant piece of work that has had multiple benefits at individual, team and institutional levels.

The purpose of the university is founded on a 'commitment to the growth of people' and it is here that I and most, if not all of my colleagues get our fulfilment from work.

A values-driven approach to service delivery

A common problem that arises in organisations is that services are often delivered based on organisational structure rather than on the customer needs. Structure should always be subordinate to process. Without entering into the 'student as consumer' debate, there is a clear need to focus on our students, especially with Bucks being a teaching-led university. In previous years, the individual departments had produced their own workshops and courses, without reference or clear linkages to what colleagues provided. Bringing together the staff from across the Directorate has led to changes that we believe recognise synergies and offer an improved and more seamless service to our students.

There is a range of different professionals working across the Directorate, including careers and guidance advisers, learning technologists, student learning developers, academic developers and an enterprise consultant. Some of these have specialist backgrounds from previous studies and roles, including in languages, teaching, accountancy, engineering, maths and nursing. While some of the Directorate staff actively teach in the more traditional sense (i.e. through designing and delivering workshops and courses, including assessment and feedback), we all support learning in one way or another. It is this student-focused approach to service delivery that is our unifying value.

A values-driven approach in practice

The vignettes and discussion below demonstrate how some of the values I have discussed are being put into practice within the Directorate, illustrating how they have enabled effective collaborative working across the different professions.

A student focus

The vignette below illustrates how this unifying value of student-centred support led to an interprofessional collaboration following a Directorate away day. It exemplifies Covey's second and third roles of leadership, path-finding and alignment. The away day had been designed partly as an opportunity to learn about each section's work, priorities and challenges, but also to enable the new teams to get to know each other and to open up discussions about working more closely together for the benefit of our students. Being physically located in different parts of the campus, most individual team members had not worked closely with each other and some of us were entirely new to the University. I regarded the day as an informal professional development opportunity.

We chose an off-site location for the away day, enabling us to feel free of our routine responsibilities and issues and to enjoy a spirit of openness, sharing, fun and learning.

Vignette one: joint working with a focus on student employability

> *Restructuring the Directorate presented opportunities for new partnerships in planning and delivering services to students. Two areas for collaboration presented themselves during the away day team presentations, when it was noted that both Careers & Employability (C&E) and the Learning Development Unit (LDU) worked with students seeking support in mathematical-reasoning psychometric tests used by employers, and in the design and content of their curriculum vitae.*
>
> *Following the Directorate away day, informal meetings were arranged between one of the careers advisers and one of the learning developers to*

find out more about their particular ways of working, the groups of students involved and the respective range of services currently offered.

Colleagues from the two departments pooled their knowledge of the help that students frequently requested and, noticing significant overlap and instances of cross-referral, agreed to collaborate on developing two sets of holistic interventions for off-the-shelf delivery at various stages of the academic year and for a variety of audiences.

The first intervention was a psychometrics workshop. The workshop combined aspects of support previously siloed in the two separate departments. It was piloted as part of the University's elective 'Activity Week' programme. C&E led with an overview of psychometric testing, examining the various test styles and their increasing importance in graduate recruitment, training and staff development planning. LDU facilitated an audit of basic numeracy skills commonly required, clarifying the tests' intended unpredictability in demanding calm but quick application of basic mathematical 'common sense' in deliberately unfamiliar workplace scenarios. The LDU's practical mathematics tasks rounded off the session, drawing on C&E's collection of sample assessments and LDU's knowledge of skill-building resources and experience in providing structured support to students with high levels of maths anxiety. The pilot was well received and the workshop is now available for tutors or groups of students to book on request.

For the second intervention, colleagues addressed the issue of students needing help to compose CVs by collaborating on four linked workshops that drew in complementary staff expertise. An initial C&E-led induction positioned the offer of online and onsite provision of the service for students' subsequent self-referral. C&E colleagues then enabled exploration of employer expectations, common CV structures, essential sections for inclusion and pitfalls to avoid. The LDU helped students to populate their chosen structure by guiding them through reflective self-audit of their strengths and motivations to develop a summary of employability skills. This was followed by practical activities to enhance use of the action-oriented, outcomes-focussed writing style. Besides stronger CVs, additional benefits to students

> included clearer self-awareness, readiness to discuss their skills objectively and confidence in analysing job descriptions. From an academic point of view, students have the opportunity to enhance their reflective skills, evidence-based writing, use of the third person, ability to adapt their writing style to different audiences, and to enrich their vocabulary. These workshops will be trialled during a pre-sessional undergraduate course, and feedback will be used to finesse the provision before roll-out to other areas of the University's support offer.

The main benefit of these examples of interprofessional collaboration is the breaking down of the silos of previous practice. Students are now given a more cohesive and coherent experience. The feedback to date has been positive and more work will continue within an ethos of continuous improvement. The initiative was managed within the resources of the team and it is anticipated that as well as enhancing student confidence and employability, the joint working will provide a more efficient service, although it is too early yet to say whether that is the case.

At the away day, we also had the opportunity to learn about the new service provision of an internal student temps agency, called BucksTemps. Directorate colleagues soon started seeing opportunities for collaboration between the teams with a win-win scenario for both staff and students.

Vignette two: learning technology ambassadors through BucksTemps

> We have allocated institutional funding to the creation of student ambassador positions to support staff and students with their use of technology in learning and teaching. While they are co-ordinated through Open4Learning (O4L), this provided a good opportunity for us to pilot our processes for our new temp agency, BucksTemps, before rolling out to other departments and the faculties. Recruitment and selection, timesheets and recording, payments and re-charges required the development of new processes. Having had successful pilots, we are now on the second stage and provide internal services to the Library, Academic Quality Department, faculties and various internal departments. The next stage will be a roll-out to external clients.

> *A particular benefit of BucksTemps has been the opportunity to work with the unsuccessful applicants, who work with a careers adviser to improve their skills and CVs in a focused way.*

The learning technology ambassadors have successfully completed one cycle of employment through the agency and the processes that were piloted have now been honed and rolled out more widely across the University. This initiative provided professional development for me and my colleagues with the main benefit being the synergies made from bringing together different professional skills to solve an institutional problem of finding appropriate students to fill the positions. An important by-product was the increased confidence in the recruitment and selection processes, resulting in the best temps for O4L as evidenced by the positive feedback gained from staff using their services. The O4L team were happy to leave the process in the hands of their professional colleagues, which enabled them to focus on their key areas of work.

More significantly, it provided an improved opportunity for our students. The successful candidates were able to develop their IT and employability skills, increase their knowledge of workplace procedures, enhance their CV with evidence of a professional work placement and earn a reasonable wage to support their learning. The unsuccessful candidates were all offered personal feedback and support in developing areas of weakness, leading to future successful temp placements. This is a benefit that would not be offered through a standard temp agency. Creating the new agency has not been without challenges, but good relationships are ensuring that these are ironed out.

Building communities

One of the key characteristics of Spears' (2002, p.4) servant leadership is about building communities. This has been critical here at Bucks in bringing together different professionals and encouraging collaborative working.

It has been greatly helped with better co-location, the first step towards which was in autumn 2014 when C&E, LDU and the new academic development team were housed in the same wing, sharing offices and student interview space and shared learning spaces. We expect to include O4L soon too, and we shall also be near the library, the Student Union and the Student Services Directorate.

The importance of the social learning spaces for staff and students is part of our building community. A shared informal space, including colourful décor, informal and formal seating arrangements and plenty of light has allowed more opportunities for networking, conversations and general relationship-building in stark contrast to a year ago with the three teams in different parts of the campus. Colleagues are sharing ideas and problem-solving within a genuine learning and teaching community. Students can find the different services more easily and can be referred on to nearby colleagues where appropriate.

The physical bringing together of the different departments of the Directorate is mirrored by the bringing together of our virtual presence. One element of this involved an exploration of how we could improve online communication with our students and other service users. Getting mixed or multiple messages from different teams from the Directorate would not be helpful and we want our students to see the service as cohesive, so we have created a cross-Directorate group to consider one aspect of this: our use of social media. Social media is of increasing importance to our communications and this is regarded as work-in-progress. Indeed, with the rapid changes in mode and means, communication is requiring increased resourcing. While social media provides opportunities for efficiencies in speed and targeting of messages, additional work was needed to ensure that the Directorate maintained a strategic, collaborative focus in our communications.

Vignette three: social media group

> *The restructure of Careers led to a creation of a 0.5 post specifically for our online communications. The post-holder has designed a user-friendly web presence for the team, and has also become our social media*

expert, pioneering its use across the Directorate and covering our range of services.

In addition, she has introduced social media workshops for C&E, Library staff, LDU and schools liaisons, enhancing the potential for the use of social media with students and staff. The workshops provide a safe space to practise new skills and approaches in order to develop a more accessible and up-to-date service for students.

As well as the communications training and up-skilling, the workshops provide a platform for sharing new and innovative practice and an opportunity to keep informed of developments across the whole institution.

One of the benefits of this collaborative approach has included the growing awareness across the institution of the services we offer to students to help them to build their employability skills, and the opportunities we provide them with access to, both internally and externally from employers who contact us to pass on vacancies.

One of our key challenges has been managing the communications in terms of volume, focus, frequency and prioritisation. The main way of meeting these challenges is through the shared University values of clarity of purpose, openness and respect, and using servant leader values of listening and persuasion. Open and respectful discussions also help to build our community networks through stronger relationships.

Empowerment

A recurrent sub-theme in this chapter has been on staff continuous professional development (CPD). To me, this is imperative to empowering our staff, as well as being essential when bringing professionals together in an environment where you hope collaboration will flourish. People need to feel confident when undertaking potentially unfamiliar roles and develop the necessary skills to undertake new activities.

We are in the process of promoting a Bucks CPD framework, based on the UK Professional Standards Framework (HEA, 2011). The UKPSF includes four values which complement our University CORD values and servant leadership values: respect individual learners and diverse learning communities; promote participation in HE and equality of opportunity for learners; use evidence-informed approaches and the outcomes from research, scholarship and CPD; acknowledge the wider context in which HE operates recognising the implications for professional practice.

While I am working on this project for the whole institution, it has a particular role for our Directorate to the extent that the HEA recognises the UKPSF as being for those who teach *and* support learning. We are using this initiative to raise our profile across the University, alongside other professional support colleagues, and to underpin our joint working as a team of diverse professionals in HE.

Vignette four: CPD framework for academics and professional services staff

> *While working on our application for HEA accreditation, I have been persuading colleagues to look at their own CPD and HEA fellowship opportunities. Bucks has around 36% staff as Fellows of the HEA, which is in line with the national average. However, to date there has been no active encouragement of non-teaching staff involvement, which we are now changing. Rita in C&E has now gained Associate Fellowship of the Higher Education Academy and other professional services staff are working on their application, including colleagues from the Library and timetabling. This isn't just about gaining HEA status, but also about an acknowledgement of contributions to supporting learning, professional credibility and breaking down barriers between academics and non-academic staff.*

Concluding thoughts

I believe that as a leader, I have a stewardship role in the care and sustainability of my team. This isn't about ownership, nor even accountability, but is more about fostering and working within a culture of respect and trust. I remain accountable for the actions and results of my team, but I genuinely believe that such a culture of respect and trust provides better lives and workplaces and ultimately better service to our students and others.

To really foster interprofessional collaboration you need to be clear about your values and to align them with the way you work across and between departments: consult and share a clear vision (i.e. 'connect with focus'); learn to support and empower your staff and students; trust your people but be there for them when they need you; and be a role model in all you do.

Acknowledgements

We thank our colleagues for ideas, input and acting as supportive and critical friends; especially Kath Dunn (Careers & Employability), Steve Hoole (Open 4 Learning), and Simon Lee-Price (Learning Development Unit).

References

Covey, S. 2002. Servant-leadership and community leadership in the twenty-first century. In: Spears, L. and Lawrence, M. eds. *Focus on Leadership: Servant-Leadership for the twenty-first century.* New York: John Wiley

Greenleaf, R.K. 1998 *The Power of servant-leadership.* San Francisco: Berrett Koehler

Higher Education Academy. 2011. *UK Professional Standards Framework.* [Online]. [Accessed 21 July 2014]. Available from: http://www.heacademy.ac.uk/ukpsf

Hussey, T. and Smith, P. 2010. *The trouble with Higher Education*. London: Routledge.

Lewin, K. 1951. *Field theory in social science; selected theoretical papers*. D. Cartwright. ed. New York: Harper & Row.

Spears, L.C. 2002. Tracing the past, present and future of servant-leadership. In: Spears, L.C. and Lawrence, M. 2002. *Focus on Leadership: Servant-Leadership for the twenty-first century*. New York: John Wiley

Critical Collaboration: a narrative account of a newly established interprofessional team.

By the UCA Canterbury Learning and Enhancement and Support Team: John Sutter*, LES Manager; Ian Badger, Teaching and Learning Librarian; Steve Dixon-Smith, Learning Development Tutor; Elaine Hatfield, Learning Support Manager; Malcolm Wallis, Dyslexia Advisor; Charlotte Kupper, Janice Rowan Careers and Employability Advisors

*For bio, please see page 173.

This chapter tells the story of the formation and development of an interprofessional team following a major restructure. It explores the development of new collaborative ways of working, the benefits of interprofessional collaboration and the challenges of bringing together different working practices, value systems and varying perspectives on the role of 'learning development'.

Background to the restructure

University for the Creative Arts (UCA) has four campuses spread across a large geographical area (Farnham, Epsom, Rochester and Canterbury). During a large scale restructure in 2012-13, two separate UCA departments - Library and Learning Services (LLS), and Student Development Services (SDS) - were combined into a single new department: Library and Student Services.

The original Library and Learning Services (LLS) team was based in the Library and included subject librarians fulfilling a fairly traditional role, as well as study advisors supporting students with the development of their academic skills. The Student Development Services unit was based outside the Library, and included three specialist services:

- Careers and Employability
- Disability Support
- English for Academic Purposes

Prior to the restructure there was some overlap of roles across the two departments, with both services sharing a remit of providing support to students. Signposting of that support was unclear, and consequently students who needed or wanted help with their studies might be routed in a number of different directions. Additionally, there was a lack of coordinated liaison with academics, so support tended to be provided discretely and at some 'distance' from the main course of study.

In the new Library and Student Services structure, the traditional subject-based librarian role became the new **Teaching and Learning Librarian.** The librarian would still support students to develop their information literacy (IL) skills but would increasingly focus their work outside of the Library, in particular exploring ways to embed IL within the curriculum. In addition, due to the overlap between the two roles, the old Library-based 'study advisors' were combined with the English for Academic Purposes tutor role to create the new role of Learning Development Tutor.

The new structure was intended to provide much clearer pathways to appropriate support for students and, of equal importance, to enable a coordinated interprofessional response to courses that would become the foundation for more embedded provision. This would allow interprofessional teams to work with academics at curriculum level to effectively embed skills development into the courses, rather than providing support only at a distance.

Previously the various roles had operated very separately, distributed across campus locations, with little interaction with professionals in the other teams. The new, more integrated campus teams would work within a shared office space that would enable them to work much more closely together. In the new department, each of the four campuses would have its own dedicated Learning Enhancement and Support (LES) team based in the campus library. To create these teams, a number of newly-defined specialist roles were brought together from the two old departments.

These were:

- Careers and Employability Advisor
- Learning Support Manager, a role that manages and coordinates support for students with disabilities.
- Dyslexia Advisor
- Teaching and Learning Librarian (TLL)
- Learning Development Tutor (LDT)

Each campus team would be managed by an on-site Learning Enhancement and Support Manager (LES manager - also a new role), who would themselves possess one of the team specialisations. The four LES managers would each lead across campus on a different specialism (disability and dyslexia / information literacy / careers and employability / language and learning development). The role therefore had a dual purpose: on the one hand to lead the local interprofessional team, and on the other to be a strategic lead for the specialism across the entire University.

This created a structure in which each colleague would effectively be a member of two teams: a local, interprofessional campus team, and a cross-campus specialist team. While the specialist lead would set the overall direction and priorities for each specialism across the University, management responsibilities would rest with the campus LES manager.

The underlying vision for the new Library and Student Services department was that the establishment of these new teams would shift provision away from 'deficit' models of support provision towards a more critical, inclusive, embedded and curriculum-facing model of enhancement that focused on working more closely with academic staff to remove barriers to student progression and achievement.

This chapter focuses on the Canterbury campus team and has been collaboratively conceived and written, but the chief narrator voice you will hear in what follows - the 'I' of the main body of text - is John's.

However, I (John) write not as a manager but as a participant colleague in a shared experience and, I hope, as a synthesising, reflective and critical voice, bringing in the voices and perspectives of other colleagues where apposite. And while some colleagues are directly quoted more than others, all have contributed extensively to the thinking and direction of this chapter.

We've grouped our reflections under seven 'lessons learnt' during our first year as a team. We have focused on the elements that seemed crucial from our own experience, and that reflect the key factors that can lead to improved and effective collaborative practice.

Morale

The first thing to understand is that we had all emerged from the restructure slightly traumatised and fragile, having spent most of the previous academic year under the considerable strain of securing our employment and wondering what the future would hold. We moved into a new open plan office in the Canterbury library in September 2014 highly relieved that this process was behind us. For the most part we were strangers, many of us having been previously based on other campuses.

However, balancing any negative feelings hanging over from the restructure, it was apparent from day one that there was also a spirit of optimism and renewed energy within the team. The new structure *did* make a lot of sense. Previously, the various specialist roles had been very remote from each other, and there was little sense of any interprofessional campus team.

The cross-campus specialist teams each seemed to work to their own notions of the 'territory' they covered. In practice this had meant that teams often operated in something of a silo, often unwittingly reproduced each other's functions. For example, study advisors, EAP tutors and librarians might all give students advice on research and/or referencing; not necessarily a bad thing in itself, but confusing for students and staff alike. More seriously, this practice often resulted in very 'generic' advice, rather than contextualised expertise.

The fact that we were now established and labelled as a campus-based interprofessional team generated its own sense of mission and purpose. The selection process for these new posts had tested the individuals' understanding of the desired inclusive and embedded model of provision, and so we each stepped into our new roles with a shared sense of purpose: we already knew what this team might be for and what we were setting out to accomplish.

This common vision and understanding was key because, whether a team bonds instantly or needs more moulding, it is important to at least have a shared sense of where you want to go. This is particularly important when bringing together different professionals who may have varying visions and values. As a manager, I seek to promote as open and 'flat' a management style as possible, giving as much responsibility and freedom to my staff as I can while always being clear about what we are trying to achieve.

We were lucky in that from day one, judging from the atmosphere of *bonhomie* and humour, it was apparent that we were going to get on well; this was clearly a team of compatible people. Of course, a team of compatible personalities in itself might not always result in productivity, but for me coming in as a manager, the openness and respect people seemed to be showing each other was exactly the soil I felt would nurture good teamwork, trust in each other's abilities, and a sense of common purpose.

Charlotte Kupper (Careers and Employability Advisor): One of the real strengths of the LES team is that we are all very approachable and open with each other, which gives us the opportunity to discuss different approaches to what we do and at times it can be very inspirational.

To foster these relationships, it was clear to me that what we would need initially as a new team was a fair amount of 'talking time' to provide the opportunity to get to know each other, and to get to know how we understood our various roles. I like to think of myself as a fairly laid-back manager; I've always felt it best to trust colleagues' expertise and judgement wherever possible and generally let them get on with things.

I see my role as primarily providing an overall steer, so it seemed that the first 'management' priority would simply be to provide good forums for talk, establish an open and informal environment, and see what happened.

Space

As well as compatible and open personalities, space probably played a key role in creating opportunities for discussion. The office space we had moved into, a newly remodelled (and attractive) open plan area inside the library, was big enough to accommodate all six of us, yet small enough for conversation to be possible across the entire space. This new space played a huge role in enabling the kind of conversations and opportunities for talk, both formal and informal, that I was so keen to encourage.

Janice Rowan (Careers and Employability Advisor): Working in closer proximity to each other lends itself to informal discussions about our individual roles and I have learnt more about disability support and learning development during this last year than I did in the previous seven. In the same role at the Rochester campus, where the LES team are still based in their original spaces, I have noticed how isolated it feels working away from them and how divorced I am from what is going on. Working in a communal space naturally lends itself to the sharing of information and at Canterbury there is a general sense that we are all working together.

As well as opening up opportunities for conscious sharing of perspective and expertise between staff, the new space created interesting and beneficial serendipities.

Janice Rowan (Careers and Employability Advisor): I had met Arthur, an autistic student, while he was doing the National Diploma at Canterbury in 2012 but had lost touch with him when he joined a degree course in Farnham in 2013. By chance, through a conversation overheard in the LES office, I learned that Arthur had become unable to continue on the course at Farnham and was trying to switch to another degree course back in Canterbury. I was able to offer my support if required; I felt that my previous contact with Arthur was invaluable as he knew me quite well and we had established a good rapport. From that point on I worked jointly with Elaine, the Learning Support Manager, to ensure that there would be both advocacy and a smoother transition for Arthur if he did get a place on the course. For me, this is a good example of how interprofessional collaboration can work well and be enhanced by working in a shared space. If Arthur had been a Rochester student I would not have informally heard about his situation and would not necessarily have been involved with helping to resolve it.

Malcolm Wallis (Dyslexia Advisor): After operating as part of a team of seven in a medium-sized open plan room within the Library for three months or so, I saw that the whole character of my job had changed. Before, I worked in an area where no student was likely to come without a problem, financial, emotional, or functional. The student had to take an unaccustomed left turn and pass through three doors to reach me. Now, I am some 12 feet away from the IT helpdesk and the dissertation booklist overnight loan shelf, and the single door is always open. In theory, I offer a drop-in service in the morning and appointments in the afternoon, but what happens most often is that someone asks for me at the Library Gateway desk and one of the treasured library assistants comes and gets me. My function has been transformed from an emergency support service to a resource: I'm no longer a sticking plaster; I'm a reference book.

Malcolm's characterisation of his function as changing from "emergency support" to "resource" is significant: the new space itself has had a role in transforming the function of the whole team in this way. It is now an identified space where students, and indeed staff, can come and find solutions to the challenges and issues they face. They may not always be clear about exactly who they need to speak to in terms of job role, but they know whoever it is will be based in that office, and that even if that particular person is not there, someone will be able to tell them who it is, make an appointment for them, or even just say "Hang on a sec, I'll go see if I can find them".

This means that students and staff also view us a team, which in turn improves lines of communication. I will now often get asked by students and staff alike "Is so-and-so around today?" in the expectation that I will know the answer, that I will be able to pass on a message, and that I will be able respond in some way if the matter is particularly urgent.

The geography of our new location, together with the serendipity of overheard conversation, also transformed our relationships with the academic teams, leading to much easier sharing of contacts and on-the-hoof collaborative planning and action. At the start of the year Adrian, one of the Fine Art tutors, came in to talk to Ian Badger (Teaching and Learning Librarian). Adrian and Ian had previously worked together on another campus, and Adrian wanted to find out if Ian might be able to run a session for his students on academic research for their dissertations. I happened to be in the office at the time, was introduced, and gave a quick overview of the new LDT role. This immediately resulted in the planning of a series of collaboratively taught sessions (Adrian, Ian and myself) for Fine Art students working towards their final dissertations. More importantly, this type of interprofessional collaboration provided an opportunity and forum for a much greater critical approach to our roles, and to our presumed functions, as will be explored in more detail under headings 4 and 5.

Even when empty, or nearly empty, the shared space also created opportunities for team working. The simple practice of using displays with photographs of the team and descriptions of their roles led to much easier cross-referral:

Malcolm Wallis (Dyslexia Advisor): Dyslexic students may need the same help that non-dyslexic students need, but may not be able to find the word to describe it; now I can show them the reference librarian's face, rather than just refer them to his title.

Of course, a shared open space can also be problematic. While there was a common desire to move away from the previous rather medical model in which all students coming to see us would automatically be judged to need a confidential space as if they were sharing something taboo or to be ashamed of, there does need to be sufficient one-to-one / small group space for more confidential conversations. Many students may not want their disability, learning difference or general need for help disclosed or discussed in a public space. We are fortunate in Canterbury to have enough small rooms available for one-to-ones. Furthermore, as a manager I would certainly benefit at times from a private office (for instance, in writing this I have occupied a one-to-one room that I will have to vacate should Steve, Elaine or one of the others suddenly need it for a tutorial). There are times when I will need to take a phone call that is confidential in nature or see a member of staff one-to-one, and these times are not always predictable.

Creating opportunities for interprofessional sharing

If the two factors discussed above - morale and space - matter, and in themselves have contributed to spontaneous and worthwhile professional discussion, so do some deliberate and planned interventions. It was clear that if we were to operate successfully as a team, we would each have a lot to learn, particularly about the nature of each other's specialisms, and an understanding of our roles.

The new job titles were problematic enough, not least in terms of keeping academics and students alert to what we each actually did. They certainly provoked impromptu office discussions along the lines of "So, um, what exactly do you do?" during the moving in process as we all unboxed books and belongings from our previous offices. But it was clear that we would need to move towards deeper understandings and negotiations of specialisms and roles.

We collectively decided to keep a space for bi-weekly team meetings on a Monday morning. As well as providing an opportunity to discuss immediate operational matters, these meetings would give us all the chance to explicitly interrogate our own and each other's specialisms. Parallel to this, we set up some mini-discussions for particular team members to discuss where there might be blurred lines between their specialisms, in terms of their roles and *modus operandi*, for example, how would the Learning Development Tutor and the Teaching and Learning Librarian work together? Who would do what in relation to a student asking for help with a dissertation?

In these meetings, the simple process of describing what we each did or thought we should be doing went a long way towards building everyone's understanding of the breadth of expertise in the team and the range of issues we might individually or collectively encounter, as well as building a real sense of ourselves as a team, rather than a collection of individuals with different specialisms. We described what we did in terms of the 'what, how and why', and so gained insight into not just the different fields of practice, but also the techniques and strategies that might be usefully shared.

Charlotte Kupper (Careers and Employability Advisor): I have gained a really good understanding of my colleagues' specialisms and this has challenged me to think more about how the students can benefit from us working together.

For Charlotte, this might mean drawing on Malcolm's expertise when giving careers advice to potentially dyslexic learners (perhaps by using more visuals in a presentation), or it might mean borrowing a technique from language teaching to help international students, such as concept-checking unfamiliar or technical vocabulary.

Theory

The Library restructure had explicitly stressed the embedding strategy of the new department. However, 'embedding' can mean very different things to different people. Is a workshop on essay writing that is timetabled as part of a Fine Arts course 'embedded', for instance? Not in my view, unless at minimum it is a) about a specific, contextualised assignment, **and** b) explores language and literacy as part of the Fine Art content of the course, rather than a separate add-on for students who 'need help with writing'. So, teasing out my new colleagues' understanding of what exactly 'embedding' meant for them would be particularly important.

Linked to this, and generative of some hugely productive conversations, was the overarching and potentially problematic Learning Enhancement and Support badging of our unit. This suggested two functions of our various roles - and possibly rather conflicting ones. How far should we be 'supporting' students and how far 'enhancing' their experience? If the stated aims of the department were to *embed* our various functions within courses, in the sense of interacting directly with the curriculum to enhance the student experience, we had to begin to think about how each specialism conceived of 'embedding', 'support' and 'enhancement', and what this might mean for specialist practice.

As a language/literacies specialist myself, I wanted to discover how similar or different my colleagues' specialist analyses of these concepts might be to my own linguistic perspective, and if the implications for practice were likewise. I decided that it would be useful, using the forum of our Monday meetings, to explicate my specialist theoretical standpoint and open it up to discussion, critique and challenge.

At this point, I should declare myself as someone with a very socially-situated view of education, and therefore with a conviction that the linguistic, literacy and semiotic demands of university are culturally constructed and ideological rather than natural or neutral. I therefore take the position (which, as I made clear to colleagues, is itself a contested one in my own field as a language specialist) that there are no 'academic conventions' (in terms of a very broad range of categories including behaviours, pedagogies, assessment and assessment criteria, ways of talking and writing, and research) that cannot be challenged and critiqued.

I first outlined a socially-situated position on 'embedding'. This was essentially that language and literacies are always context-dependent and cannot really be analysed or understood outside of the context.

This means that 'content' and 'language' are not truly separable, which in turn implies that 'generic' models of language 'support', where for instance students are taught academic writing outside of their main course, stand little chance of really understanding the real language use of a real context.

Steve Dixon-Smith (Learning Development Tutor): An example of this came up in a discussion I had with an overseas Fine Art student asking for help with writing an artist's statement:

Student: what do they mean when they ask me: what kind of dialogue do you want to establish with your audience?

LDT: well… a dialogue is a kind of conversation, so they want to know what kind of conversation you want to have with your audience.

Student: I know a dialogue is a conversation, but what do they mean when they say it?

Steve's point here is that 'dialogue' means something very special in this particular context, and something that is not easily transmitted outside of it. In fact, although commonplace in many Western art contexts, 'dialogue' or 'conversation' could be considered to be rather strange metaphors to use about artist/audience relationships. In what ways does the audience speak back to artists? In many ways, monologue might seem more intuitively appropriate. Artists send their work out into the world, or display it, but it's not immediately clear that an audience can 'talk back', unlike, say, in the case of an improvising jazz musician, where some kind of two-way interaction with an audience might be more intuitively understandable. So 'dialogue' is not just a metaphor here; it's an entire discourse, a whole way of thinking about art, artists and audiences that is neither neutral nor transparent, but grounded in a particular culture and context.

So, for me as a language specialist at least, 'embedding' means locating moments such as these where 'content' and language are effectively meshed together, and turning these into learning opportunities for students by making them explicit within the main provision of the course, rather than as an 'add-on' or 'support'. This means the language specialist and course tutor working together, bringing their joint expertise to bear on the curriculum.

This sort of collaborative working (and collaborative teaching) is enhancement rather than support. And while some support will always be necessary, this is a vision of learning development that is properly inclusive. It focuses not on 'needy' students but on the curriculum itself, so that our primary activity is about ***identifying** and removing barriers to student achievement* rather than merely removing barriers to student achievement

These early expositions and discussions of approach and theory bore immediate fruit; it was made very explicit just how much the team agreed. We all in fact aspired to such an 'embedded enhancement' model, and could all produce theory from our specialisms to support it. Elaine and Malcolm, for instance, subscribed to the social model of dyslexia / disability:

We challenge the deficit models of dyslexia in favour of a social model that maintains that we are not 'disabled' by our dyslexia, but by the expectations of the world we live in. There is nothing 'wrong' with being dyslexic per se. We would argue that dyslexia is an experience that arises out of natural human diversity on the one hand and a world on the other where the early learning of literacy, and good personal organisation and working memory is mistakenly used as a marker of 'intelligence'. The problem here is seeing difference incorrectly as 'deficit' (RossCooper, 2006).

In so many ways this parallels what language and literacy theorists now have to say about linguistic differences and ideology (e.g. Pennycook, 2001; Gee , 2008; Jenkins, 2014). Particular varieties of English and particular literacy practices come to be (arbitrarily) privileged in many settings, including academic ones (Benesch, 2001). For instance, should we be trying to get all students to conform to 'standard academic English' (should such a thing actually exist), or work towards more linguistically inclusive environments? Taking student writing as one example, spelling, grammar and lexis are all extra challenges that assignments can bring to dyslexic learners or to students who speak English as an additional language, or to those who speak an English that does not conform to 'academic convention'.

Many linguists such as Jenkins see very good reasons for questioning and challenging these conventions:

'As an external examiner of PhD candidates, I have started checking respective universities' websites, and (regardless of their geographical setting) if they proclaim themselves to be 'international' or 'global', ignore all intelligible non-native English in the thesis, and add the following to my examiner's report: "Note that my policy in assessing work in universities that present themselves as international is to request revisions only where an item is potentially unintelligible to an international readership, not merely where something differs from native English". I hope it will not be long before many others follow suit'. (Jenkins, 2014, p.76)

Meanwhile, after a team meeting discussion about information literacy theory, Ian Badger (TLL) gave me a book to read (Lloyd, 2010) that takes a very similar theoretical orientation to his specialism, a socially-situated practices view informed by many of the same writers who feed into the linguistics literature. Ian and I discussed how the things that students do or need to do in terms of information literacy can, just as in my own field, be seen as a set of highly contextualised practices located in particular settings, geographical and virtual locations as opposed to a set of 'skills'. On this reading, the role of the TLL would be to help students to understand, critique and participate effectively in these practices (just as, say, in the practice of academic writing). The role itself becomes one of critique and enquiry (e.g. finding out how 'research' for a fine artist might involve different orientations and practices to 'research' as conducted by an architect), rather than the mere passing on of a set of generic and apparently unproblematic 'skills'. The field of the information literacy specialist becomes one of social relations and identities, the playing out and establishment of power relations, together with a critiquing of 'information' and 'knowledge' in subject-specific and library contexts. This is very similar to the orientation of the LDT role, the taking up of a critical perspective on issues of social and power relations in teaching, learning and assessment contexts.

And with Charlotte, we talked about the tension between the 'skills' view of learning typically held in the business world or a 'careers' context, and again the emerging, more social orientation of current thinking about the world of work. This isn't a tension completely resolved in practice yet, (for instance, a 'skills' audit is a common technique in a careers advice context) but it has given us at least one avenue of critical exploration.

Theory isn't enough on its own: a shared ethos of practice matters too.

As well as our shared theoretical perspectives, it was also apparent that much of the mainstream day-to-day practice across all specialisms seemed to be about helping students hurdle barriers rather than removing them. Of course much of this (especially in the case of disability) has been driven by funding, how the DSA has worked, and undoubtedly for all specialisms, by the historical academic practices of the University community. As a team we quickly developed effective sharing of practice, a system of student referral and interprofessional working:

Elaine Hatfield (Learning Support Manager): Graham, who has autism, had unexpectedly enrolled onto the BA (Hons) Graphic Design at UCA Canterbury having completed the two year Extended National Diploma Course, but had been advised by his tutors that he may not be ready to undertake a degree course.

After failing the first unit Graham was very anxious, but as it transpired, only 9 of the 1st year students had passed the unit. The LDT and TLL stepped in with a workshop to assist students to understand the semiotics underpinning the design brief for this unit.

People with autistic spectrum conditions (ASC) often interpret language very literally due to their logical reasoning, therefore understanding nuances and subtlety of language can be a minefield where mistakes lead to a retreat from situations and interactions that can be ambiguous or unpredictable. Neurological differences of people with ASC can also affect sensory and social perceptions, having an impact on their experiences of everyday life. This can lead to gaps in developmental understanding and knowledge retention. In Graham's case, he was not able to make the linguistic connections implied in the brief due to lack not only of cultural references, but also of opportunities to learn from life experience.

Steve Dixon-Smith (Learning Development Tutor): My involvement with Graham came out of Ian's (TLL) discussion with Elaine (LSM) about what had initially appeared to be a research difficulty, but had transpired to be a difficulty in responding to the assessment brief. Elaine explained that limited social interaction means that autistic students can struggle to realise the interpretations expected of them by others. She also mentioned that she'd previously observed EFL [English as a foreign language] classes and thought how useful the teaching approach might be for autistic students.

With this in mind, Ian and I met Graham weekly to work on his resubmission and forthcoming written assessment. Ian was able to help Graham find research materials that he could get enthusiastic about, and I would try to elicit ways in which they could be useful. The language teaching techniques of breaking down the meaning of the task, checking understanding and eliciting responses from which Graham could make better sense of the assignment did seem to help. However, bridging the gap between the world Graham experiences and the one he's being introduced to as a Graphic Design student would have been impossible without Tom, Graham's LSA, illuminating the occasional blind alleys I would lead us down in our search for meaning. It struck me that Tom had in-depth knowledge about things I didn't, but that were necessary to make the assessment meaningful to Graham, including the course, graphic design as a discipline, autism and, most importantly, Graham.

Elaine Hatfield (Learning Support Manager): So Graham was able to resit and pass the unit. Graham says that he still finds the writing difficult but has learned with the help from the TLL and LDT to be more independent in his research.

Cross collaboration and sharing knowledge of both ASC and linguistic barriers to learning between the team led to a better understanding not only for us but also for Graham, his support worker and the academic staff.

This is a clear example of how collaborative interprofessional work helped a student pass an assignment, but one that is also an example of 'support' rather than 'enhancement'; the kind of approach in fact that our shared theoretical perspective was questioning, an example of 'support' with an interesting sting in its tail:

Steve Dixon-Smith: Collaboration between roles brought about a rich network of support for Graham, without which he almost certainly wouldn't have passed, but it also raised some important questions about the assessment itself. When quizzed about the content of his essay by his tutor, Graham wasn't able to reproduce the arguments he'd made. This led to questions over whether sufficient learning had taken place despite his passing the essay. Discussions within the LES team centred around whether this pointed to a problem with Graham's learning or with essayist, outcome-focussed assessment design more generally.

Malcolm Wallis: With effort, determination and skilled support, a lot of dyslexic students can put together something very like a dissertation. However, my observation is that though they eventually give what teachers ask for, they may not always receive what teachers hope to give.

As a team, we were coming to see that we shared a common *ethical* view of what we should be trying to achieve, a view that hinged in the end on the centrality of an inclusive approach to education, and the removal of barriers that discriminate against some students who may typically be labelled 'dyslexic', 'disabled', 'speakers of English as an additional language' or 'widening participation'.

Collaboration beyond the immediate team

The example described above revealed that collaborative working could only go so far if it was limited to collaboration *within our team*.

We had to move towards establishing collaborative working practices with colleagues in the wider University, especially those working at curriculum level. In preparation for this, we began to devote meetings, both as a whole team and in smaller groups or pairs, to sharing and identifying the most common reasons students came to us for support, and whether we could re-interpret these requests for 'support' as opportunities to enhance courses by removing or at the very least challenging barriers.

For example, the *extra* challenge presented to some dyslexic (and other) learners by particular genres of extended writing meant that there is a very high demand for learning development support in dissertation units. For students who are 'declared' as 'disabled', there already exists the 'reasonable adjustment' route, which can lead to highly enabling changes in teaching and learning or assessment methods. But this route is unavailable for students who do not neatly fit into, or decline, a category of 'disability'. What our ethos now demanded was collaborative team work, with support provided by specialists of all stripes, to work towards curriculum change that could benefit *all* students. It seemed to us that the dissertation experience could be enhanced, without in the least compromising its rigour, if there were a greater choice of assessment strategies. If we could work effectively with course leaders and tutors, we ought to be able to find ways to offer students a much wider choice of modalities for assessment, for instance through video, web-based multimedia or presentations, all of which are highly relevant to and representative of the broader changes taking place in society and with communication.

Malcolm Wallis (Learning Support Manager): Dyslexic students are as willing as their peers, but for some reason they need a different direction. No quantity of spelling rules, paragraphing techniques, voice-to-text or text-to-voice software can replace the key ingredient: permission to do it their way, which equates in the long run to permission to do their best.

Such changes would put the social model mentioned above into practice, changing the environment in such a way that categories like 'disabled', 'dyslexic' or 'second language speaker' become less definitive:

Malcolm Wallis (Learning Support Manager): The word ['dyslexia'] is wearing out its usefulness: if a tree falls but no-one is required to spell deciduous, does anyone in the forest have dyslexia? Once the ramps and automatic doors are put in place, some wheelchair users may find they scarcely need the word disabled any more, at least not at college, and for many dyslexic students the ramps and doors take the form of a simple understanding on the part of lecturers that they are not being awkward, lazy or obtuse; that this is the way their mind works.

Equally, the way learning and course content is delivered in units such as the dissertation could probably itself better address the diversity of the student demographic.

Malcolm Wallis (Learning Support Manager): The problem, if it is a problem, remains: different people take in, process and produce information in different ways. What if the teacher could find other ways to explain? What if they cut the subject into smaller or differently-shaped chunks - or bigger ones? Surely there's a way to get round the problem?

So we now began to see 'collaboration' very inclusively: within the first semester of the new team being established, we had forged strong links with the academic departments and teams on our campus. We found tutors and course leaders were often highly sympathetic to our approach, and many shared our perspectives on inclusivity and academic practices. In fact, a dissertation unit was one of our first collaborative successes: the dissertation workshop for Fine Art mentioned near the beginning of this chapter directly led to conversations with Adrian, the tutor, about the possibility of a choice of assessment modes for all, not just 'disabled' students, and then to a series of meetings with Sophia, the Fine Art course leader (who herself proved to be highly enthusiastic about this approach), and finally to a *jointly* worked-out new unit that does indeed offer all students the chance to submit in alternative modes (or a mix of them). This led to the setting up of new co-taught embedded sessions on the unit that make explicit the issues around language and literacy, multimodal communication, research and library practices that many students encounter during their dissertation.

'Upwards' discourse, institutional reflection and buy-in

It is impossible to overestimate the importance of the conversations and sharing of perspectives we had internally as a team during those first few weeks and months. It enabled us to develop a common theorised approach, and then to consider what practices within our team and the University needed to be changed or challenged. We are now able to collaborate with each other in interprofessional ways, and to collaborate with the campus academic teams to start making 'ground-up' improvements.

But as with any university, some outcomes need to be pursued at institutional levels too.

Beyond the local, we have encountered institutional barriers that currently limit the effectiveness of what we can do, and it is clear that we need to focus as much on challenging these barriers as on the 'on the ground' work we do with subject tutors and students. For instance, in the same year that we helped the schools of Fine Art and later Architecture to develop new units that allowed a choice of assessment modes for dissertation students, we also saw a key University committee bring in a new 'standard' dissertation unit that insists on a *written* outcome. This did not negate the units we had developed, but perhaps had the effect of devaluing them in the eyes of some students as an 'alternative' choice.

While we could certainly collaborate, reflect and critique with local course teams, we now realised that the (often difficult) questions we were asking also needed to be directed upwards and discussed at committee level through my own role as lead for language and learning development.

Such questions included:

- Why does this learning outcome specify a written outcome?
- What other modes might satisfy the criteria?
- What is meant by 'does this learning outcome specify a written outcome?
- What other mode, and what could count, as research?
- What does it mean linguistically to internationalise the curriculum?

Some aspects of inclusive, collaborative practice (such as offering choice of assessment modes to all students, consistent and coherent learning outcomes and criteria across courses, and inclusive validation procedures) need a wider institutional remit and cultural change, and some 'top-down' endorsement by committees, faculties, academic boards and senior management. We could also see that for this to happen effectively, our roles in a 'professional' department need to be explicitly understood as *academic* in their involvement in curricula and pedagogy, and that in particular the underpinning of education by issues of diversity, language, 'literacy' and power needed to be addressed and highlighted to the University community.

Conclusion

So where are we up to now? Locally, we've made some big strides on our Canterbury campus. As a team we're currently embedded in just about all of the courses on our campus, and are now beginning to influence and affect the planning of assignments and writing of briefs, and are co-delivering content with many tutors. We're beginning to play a meaningful role in unit and course validations. This means we're able to work with students and lecturers at unit level to really tease out contextualised opportunities for embedded enhancement of the student experience, and to win over hearts and minds on the bigger issues. At the time of writing, hearteningly we've also begun to make inroads into the some of the key University committees that discuss and affect teaching, learning and assessment. Recent changes mean that I'm now able to promote 'enhancement' and embedded approaches, and the specialist knowledge of my team, at the Inclusivity Working Group, the Teaching and Learning Committee and at Academic Board levels. This has come at a time, perhaps fortuitously, when the University is thinking carefully about and planning for the potential changes to the DSA next year, changes that themselves (especially in terms of 'anticipatory adjustments') may very well be a driver for exactly the kind of embedded enhancement approach the Canterbury LES team has been advocating. At the very least, we are sure that the collaborative work and sharing that has taken place between specialisms during this last year has resulted in a far more unified, coherent, persuasive and, we believe, effective advocacy for a truly inclusive approach to university education.

References

Baron-Cohen, S. 2008 *Autism and Asperger Syndrome: The facts.* Oxford: Oxford University Press.

Benesch, S. 2001 Critical English for academic purposes. Oxon: Routledge

Cooper, R. 2006. A social model of Dyslexia. *Language Issues.* **18**(2).

Gee, J.P. 2008. Social linguistics and literacies: Ideology in discourses. Oxon: Routledge

Jenkins, J. 2014. English as a lingua franca in the international university: The politics of academic English language policy. Oxon: Routledge.

Kress, G. 2010. Multimodality: A social semiotic approach to contemporary communication. Oxon: Routledge

Lloyd, A. 2010. Information literacy landscapes: Information literacy in eduaction, workplace and everyday contexts. Oxford: Chandos.

Pennycook, A. 2001. Critical applied linguistics: a critical introduction. Oxon: Routledge

Terms of reference: working together to develop student citation practices

By Kim Shahabudin and Helen Hathaway

About the authors

Kim Shahabudin is a Study Adviser at the University of Reading, supporting students at all levels of study in developing their academic literacies. She has been involved in learning development at a national level since 2006, serving as a member of the LearnHigher CETL and the Association of Learning Development in Higher Education (ALDinHE) Steering Group. She notes that having a co-author on the other side of an office wall is considerably easier than her last co-authoring experience with a colleague in Australia. She is a Senior Fellow of the Higher Education Academy.

Helen Hathaway has been the Information Skills Co-ordinator and Convenor of the Information Skills Group in the University of Reading Library since 1996. In this role she has reviewed the teaching, learning and assessment provision across the Library, aligning plans to University teaching priorities and concentrating on information and digital literacy. Since January 2014 she has also taken on the newly created post of Head of Academic Liaison and Support, managing liaison teams including Study Advice and Maths Support and developed a particular interest in joint working. She is a University Teaching Fellow and Senior Fellow of the Higher Education Academy.

Introduction

This chapter focuses on the practical experience of library, learning development and English for Academic Purposes (EAP) academic staff at the University of Reading in building a coordinated and collaborative approach to supporting student referencing practices. The discussion draws on the authors' experience as members of a collaborative project team comprising four members with three distinct professional roles: librarian, learning developer and EAP academic tutor. Following a brief introduction to contextualise the discussion, we describe how the team came together, analyse the difficulties of interprofessional working that we encountered and describe how we responded to these. We then elaborate on the key aspects of our research processes, external and internal networking and development of resources, focusing in each section on the ways that collaboration and co-working offer potential and actual benefits in supporting student success at university. We conclude that the outcomes of the project included not only the practical development and dissemination of joint guidance and teaching materials, but also an increased understanding among the different professions of areas of professional expertise and opportunities for co-working.

As university teaching practices and student demographics change, there has been an increasing emphasis on the value of academic skills teaching and support in UK higher education (Cottrell, 2013). Factors including the growth of the international student population, the massification of higher education, and an emphasis on league tables that may detract from the development of independent study skills at A-level, have contributed to produce a new kind of student cohort, less likely to be fully prepared for university study in the very particular academic culture of the UK (HEFCE, 2014; Whittaker, 2008; Blythman and Orr, 2002). At the same time, larger teaching groups and an increase in the number of academic tutors on part-time or sessional contracts can mean that there is less time available for tutors to offer support (Thomas and Hixenbaugh, 2006). The resulting gap threatens to leave some students disadvantaged and at risk of not fulfilling their academic potential.

Both library professionals and learning developers have key roles to play in this new learning landscape. Their respective areas of expertise in information and academic literacies cover between them the key skills needed for successful independent learning at university. These include the ability to search for, select and evaluate sources; the communication of knowledge in an appropriate, focused and critical style; and the self-management of reading, references and deadlines (Andretta, 2005; Cottrell, 2013). Teaching and support for these skills is much in demand, both from individual students and from academic departments who increasingly recognise the greater effectiveness of skills support that is discipline-specific and embedded within subject modules (Wingate, 2006; Appleton, 2005; Durkin and Main, 2002). Library professionals and learning developers have different but complementary roles to play in teaching these skills. For example, when teaching aspects of referencing, the former are trained in developing the information literacy practices needed to find, evaluate and record sources, while the latter are able to expertly demonstrate the role that these sources play in academic writing.

There is a trend for the two professions to find themselves physically co-located in a process of convergence, with learning hubs, writing centres and 'one-stop shops' bringing together support services in many university libraries (Melling, 2013; Hanson, 2005; Roberts, 2005). While this might appear to those outside of the professions to be a natural fit, a closer look would reveal differences in working practices and professional philosophies (Roberts, 2005). However these differences can, if managed with sensitivity and mutual respect, produce creative collaborations that can help us to meet the increase in demand for support and to maximise the effectiveness of teaching activities.

In an integrated service, a collectivist approach would see all staff performing similar sets of tasks, working towards a common purpose. When previously separate services or teams are integrated, this can create anxiety among staff asked to perform new tasks. Integrating separate professional services can be additionally difficult because of the differences in professional cultures.

However, taking a modified collectivist approach, by identifying common goals but also defining areas of expertise and overlap, offers a key to effective co-working between different professions. Increased co-working also has the effect of growing understanding about other professional roles, with a concomitant benefit for effective co-referral. In our institution, the learning development service is provided centrally by a small Study Advice Team which relocated in August 2011 (both physically and structurally) from Student Services to the Library. Although there were obvious alignments between the two services, the potential challenges inherent in their integration were also recognised. As well as different underpinning philosophies and ways of working, there was a need to retain the benefit of two separate 'brands', each of which had built a strong and valued identity with both students and academics, while finding ways to move towards a closer alignment.

A gradual approach to integration was adopted, starting with a relatively hands-off management approach that allowed both services time to find out how the other service worked, and how they could introduce more co-working. The service was then situated within the remit of a new Head of Academic Liaison and Support, recognising the ever-growing importance of the Library as an academic partner, and the strategic role Study Advice had to play in this. Referencing soon emerged as a key area where services overlapped and demand for guidance had increased. The chance to take part in a project on this topic, involving members of staff from the Library, Study Advice and academic faculty, offered an opportunity to develop a model of collaborative practice that could inform and motivate future integration and alignment.

The practice of correct and accurate referencing lies at the heart of academic study, yet it is regularly reported as an area fraught with difficulties for students (Neville, 2010). These difficulties can have lasting and substantial effects, with unintentional plagiarism and academic misconduct cases damaging or even ending a student's academic career (Tennant et al, 2007). With the introduction of rising tuition fees, more students (particularly international students) are challenging the results of misconduct hearings, which creates additional costs and potential reputational damage for institutions. (Office of the Independent Adjudicator, 2013). However, a survey of the advice given both at department level and at a central level (through university websites, for instance) suggests that support for referencing is often treated as simply a matter of demonstrating a set of rules and formulae for recording in a mechanistic way the bibliographical details of sources in a given order. Without a proper understanding of the principles of referencing, including when and how to build references into their writing, students may format their citations perfectly and still be open to charges of unintentional plagiarism or poor academic practice.

In the following sections, we describe our experience of collaborative working on the referencing project, showing the planned and unexpected ways in which interprofessional working helped to achieve a successful outcome to the project, and enabled us to move forward into further collaborations in the future. The project, which ran from September 2012 to July 2013, aimed to research, collate and develop effective teaching materials on referencing. We named it *'What did I do wrong?'* after the bewildered response of a student who had been accused of plagiarism.[1] The final outcome consisted of a suite of teaching materials for EAP academic tutors, which contained evaluated teaching and support resources (existing and new, internal and external) brought together through single editing and visual coherence. Guidance for adapting and using them in subject teaching was also offered.

---

[1] For more information on the project see http://blogs.reading.ac.uk/engage-in-teaching-and-learning/2012/11/28/what-did-i-do-wrong-researching-student-referencing-practices-by-helen-hathaway-clare-nukui-dr-kim-shahabudin-and-dr-liz-wilding/, http://blogs.reading.ac.uk/engage-in-teaching-and-learning/2013/04/05/what-did-i-do-wrong-supporting-independent-learning-practices-to-avoid-plagiarism-by-helen-hathaway/ and http://blogs.reading.ac.uk/engage-in-teaching-and-learning/2013/06/19/teaching-students-how-to-use-references-a-speaker-and-a-toolkit-by-dr-kim-shahabudin-helen-hathaway-clare-nukui-dr-liz-wilding/.

We had developed the understanding that support for referencing needed to go beyond the usual provision of formatting examples, and in recognition of this, we named the resource *The Academic Integrity Toolkit*.

It was launched in June 2013, and has received very positive feedback from tutors and senior staff across the University and further interest externally.[2]

Bringing different professions together

The *'What did I do wrong?'* project was originally an imposed collaboration. Having each applied individually for funding for small projects, the funding committee saw an opportunity to bring the three professions (librarian, learning developer and English for Academic Purposes (EAP) academic tutor) together to work on a larger funded project on an area of increasing concern: the development of independent learning practices needed to avoid plagiarism. The rationale in bringing together this combination of personnel was that we were all stakeholders in providing support for referencing and avoiding plagiarism. Librarians had traditionally advised on formatting citations and finding bibliographic details; learning developers taught the principles of using references in academic writing; the EAP academics were familiar with the alternative academic cultures that might lead international students into unintentional plagiarism. As a team, therefore, we could offer a diverse range of perspectives on the project's focus.

---

[2] Presentations on the project were given at the *2013 Annual Conference*, Association of Librarians and Information Specialists in the Social Sciences (ALISS) Senate House, University of London (April 2013); *2013 Annual Conference*, Librarians' Information Literacy Annual Conference (LILAC), University of Manchester (July 2013); *2013 Annual Conference*, Association of Learning Developers in Higher Education (ALDinHE), University of Plymouth (March 2013); and *'From the road less travelled to the information super highway: information literacy in the 21st Century'*, M25 Consortium/CILIP Information Literacy Group, British Library (January 2014).

There is space and need within a university community for many different professional roles. While these have often been separated into 'research', 'teaching' and 'support' roles, in truth all three types of activity are undertaken by most professions to a greater or lesser extent. For instance, reflective and evaluative practice may be construed as research, while feedback on assignments can operate as support.

In almost all professional interactions with students there is an element of teaching, though the traditional hierarchies that separate staff on academic contracts from other professional staff can obscure this. Despite these commonalities though, it is also important to recognise the boundaries of professional expertise and practice, and the professions' different motivations and working philosophies (Belzowski et al., 2013).

For instance, while both librarians and learning developers have a teaching role, some basic philosophies of libraries might draw on the notions of collecting, classifying, conserving and disseminating, principles of control and order possibly leading to a conservative and cautious approach. The focus of learning development is found in another direction, putting the emphasis on individual development and creative synergies (Hilsdon, 2011). Of course most librarians would not recognise themselves in this simplification (see CILIP, 2013 for a fuller definition of professional competencies), and not all learning developers will tend towards impractical arrays of options, but collaborators need to be aware of potential differences in approach. This is before even starting to think about the principles that governed the roles of our EAP colleagues, or the varying principles that underpin such contrasting academic disciplines as, for instance, food science and film studies (Becher and Trowler, 2001). So bringing together project team members from three different professional viewpoints might be a risky venture, with inherent difficulties arising from a lack of shared working practices, purposes and goals.

Challenges

An early difficulty we had to face arose from the different rhythms of our working years. These produced practical issues around the timing of meetings and project planning, with our EAP colleagues having their busiest periods over the summer at which time the Library and Study Advice services experience less demand, while the autumn term is busy for all. Fortunately our funding enabled us to appoint a research officer who was able to conduct the primary research with students and staff that needed to be accomplished during term time to take advantage of the participants' availability.

By simultaneously allocating small writing and research tasks, everyone remained involved in the project, even over the busiest times for their day-to-day roles. There might be a tendency in interprofessional co-working to play down differences between team members in an attempt to treat everyone equally. However, this risks creating later resentment if team members are unable to participate equally at all times. By identifying and acknowledging these tensions from the start, we were able to plan for them and find ways to ensure that no single team member was excluded or over-stretched throughout.

Communication was also a potential source of difficulty. With Study Advice located in the Library, while our other team members were on a different part of campus (and often in a different country), there was a danger that a division might develop between the two differently located sets. While setting up a workable communications strategy from the start is common advice on effective team-working, it is easy to assume that the ease of access of virtual communication makes this the best tool for the job. In fact, we found a combination of face-to-face and virtual working gave us the space for both relatively unbounded creative and social interactions, as well as more limited and controlled (and accessible) virtual communications. The importance of including some informal communications to build relationships between co-workers can be overlooked in a time-pressured working environment, but it is often the space where strengths and preferences are most easily and productively identified (Dennis and Robert, 2009). In our dual approach, a wiki was set up to store documents and facilitate collaboration on aspects like survey design and analysis. In addition to this, we held regular brief face-to-face update and brainstorming meetings. These sessions often proved to be the most creative and productive parts of the research process, acting as a slingshot to process and propel work on to the next stage. The wiki was especially useful during the development of the teaching materials, as versions were posted, commented on, edited and stored in one easily accessible location (Fig. 1). This helped to create a feeling of shared ownership of the finished materials (Walsh, 2010).

Making notes and keeping good records	Good practice; which details to note; how this helps to avoid plagiarism.	I think these could be reordered starting with the higher level activities like beginning with questions or seeking solutions. *Done KS* I think one problem for some weaker students is that they DON'T take notes - they just copy and paste information from online sources. Is it worth making an explicit statement that making notes is not the same as using the ctrl+c key in the first paragraph? *Have added KS*	Clare Liz
Building references into your writing	Using direct quotes, paraphrasing and mentions; exercises and answers.	I like this but I think there is scope for a more simplified version for students with weaker language skills. *This might be something we need to discuss. Perhaps Clare and Liz could edit some simplified versions of key topics for the Blackboard site? KS. Yes good idea* Sentence to be edited - something seems wrong: Paraphrasing takes an idea that you originally found in a source and explain it in your own words. *Edited - thank you KS*	Liz
How to précis	Example-led description of précising and when it might be used.	I think this is less useful in general and quite a high level skill. *I don't mind losing this from the Toolkit - we'll keep it in our screencast as we often have to advise students doing lit reviews on this. KS.*	Clare
How to paraphrase	Example-led description of paraphrasing; tips for better paraphrasing; exercise and answers.	Is there a way to add a section on WHY/WHEN to paraphrase (rather than give a quotation)? I think students have difficulty with both why and how. *included in 'Building refs in your writing' KS.* I think here it is important to point out that we start researching with questions we want to find answers to or alternative viewpoints and when we read we take notes on these things. We skim and scan and write down key points as they supprt or refute our hypothesis. The sample texts could come with some questions, as	Liz

Figure 1: Using a wiki for collaborative editing.

The face-to-face discussions were also vital in addressing another challenge, that of building our understanding of the extent and limits of our respective expertise and experiences. While general staff induction sessions may provide information on the various services and job roles in an institution, they are often context-neutral. Our meetings and brainstorming sessions gave us the opportunity to develop a contextualised understanding of how different types of professional interaction (with students and other staff) produced and used information that contributed to a single goal. Pressures on our time meant that meetings were often held over lunchtime; they tended to be more informal, giving us a chance to build more social relationships and trust. This is not to endorse lunchtime meetings! However, finding ways to create a more informal atmosphere, perhaps sometimes meeting over coffee, or in a venue that is not a teaching room or office, can encourage more open interactions. This was important because it meant that each team member was able to be honest in their evaluative discussions, and removed some of the barriers that institutional silos can instil (Wenger, 1998; Dennis and Robert, 2009). It built not only understanding but also respect for the roles played by different professions in a university economy by illustrating them in practice as well as in theory, and showing the pressures that every sector of university staff can experience at times.

This informal interaction additionally led to the discovery that any concerns over a lack of shared purposes and goals would prove to be unfounded.

In educational research, it is more usual for a team to come together because of shared interests before planning to undertake a project. As an 'engineered' team, we more closely resembled a student group work project than an academic project team, tasked with a project not of our making, with other team members not of our choosing. There was a certain amount of cautiousness at the start of the project, with each team member being unsure of what the others were expecting or hoping for from the research, and what roles might emerge from the group.

As a consequence, we did not start by deciding on a work plan and allocating roles. Instead we spent more time in informal discussions about our experiences of working with students to support referencing practices, what we thought might be the probable causes of student difficulties, and what sort of interventions we had already experienced success with.

This more tentative exploratory approach at the start of the project, explained by Dennis and Robert (2009) as the transition from swift trust to knowledge-based trust, helped us to identify shared goals and theories and created a common sense of purpose. Thus the most important element for the success of our collaboration was settled as a result of our response to the potential difficulties.

Interpreting research through collaboration

In the successful completion of the *'What did I do wrong?'* project, the diversity of professional identities offered a creative interpretative bonus from the start. The proposed original outcome of the project was to collate existing resources produced by individual authors at our institution and disseminate them across the University for use in teaching. However, following our early discussions and initial research, this aim was revised. We swiftly decided that the project needed to go further to be truly effective; we would need to conduct research with students from all demographics, academic staff and support services to get a clear picture of needs and concerns, and then to adapt and develop new materials that responded to those concerns.

In taking the decision to radically change the aims of the project, we drew on our different professional approaches and interactions with students. Traditionally, the Library's approach had been to focus referencing guidance on citation formatting for different textual materials and the use of EndNote as a tool to support referencing and record keeping. Teaching also took place through small group workshops or in joint sessions with study advisers, with individual support provided through one-to-one meetings with the liaison librarian for the subject who would have experience of the kinds of materials typically used. Support from the learning development service had concentrated more on group and individual teaching about the *use* of references: when citations should be included, and how references to research could be built into academic writing. The EAP academic tutors had experience of teaching both individual students and groups whose previous educational experiences were informed by quite different academic cultures to that found in the UK.

Their teaching was in the context of dedicated study skills sessions, as well as contextualised academic writing and feedback on assignments. Pooling and reviewing these three different types of student-staff interaction, we were able to draw out shared concerns and meta-issues. In particular, we recognised the importance of teaching principles rather than just practices, and that more specific support for international students could not be produced without investigating and understanding the needs and concerns of all students.

Our professional practice also dictated the decision that we would take a more explicitly research-informed approach to evaluating and developing resources. This might be obvious in the case of the EAP academic tutors, for whom research played an assumed part in their professional activities. In learning development too, advice given to students on academic writing has a strong emphasis on the need for authoritative evidence to support conclusions, while librarians spend much of their time enabling research through resource provision and organisation, as well as training users.

Consequently we were very aware that members of all of our professional communities would be more likely to receive the final resources positively if we could show that we had sound research to inform our decisions.

As part of our initial scoping research, we surveyed undergraduate students and academic staff at the University via brief email questionnaires with open text questions and face-to-face interviews. This early research indicated that few new undergraduates had a clear understanding of referencing practices at university: when, how and why references are used. In the student survey, only 4 of 75 respondents stated that they had had no problems with referencing at university, while academic staff noted misunderstandings persisting right through to the final years of an undergraduate course. This could be due to what is widely perceived as inconsistency in marking, assessment and the seriousness with which errors are treated. In addition, a pervasive problem for students in understanding referencing was the lack of a single consistent source of guidance. Where tutors were concerned about student referencing, their response tended to be to individually produce guidance for students on their own modules.

While this was well-meant (and produced many good practice examples) it often added to the confusion of students already accessing a plethora of advice from different sources. However, there were some excellent examples of innovative practice in the individual guidance material we collected that moved beyond the provision of example citations.

While imposing greater consistency in assessment was beyond the scope of the project, it was clear that we could do something about improving the consistency of guidance. The original project aim of simply collating diverse teaching and support material that had originally been produced for quite different student cohorts, discipline requirements and purposes, would not result in the kind of consistency that students currently felt was lacking. At the same time, our own individual experiences of teaching (between us) students in all the subject disciplines offered at the University had made us aware of the differences in styles and uses of referencing and the materials used.

This prompted one of the key principles in developing the toolkit resources, to give them consistency through writing style, format and visual appearance but simultaneously make them as adaptable to different disciplines as possible in content and format. This need for individual disciplines to adapt them for their own needs dictated that the materials be presented as mediated teaching materials, rather than as self-access support resources for students.

It also became apparent that a lack of understanding of the purposes and principles of referencing tended to make students dependent on examples and the security of authoritative advice. This detracted from the independent learning practices that we wanted to encourage to avoid unintentional plagiarism. Poor time management could also be a factor in encouraging errors. Our conclusion was that referencing needs to be taught as part of a package of linked independent learning practices rather than a standalone skill, and that the best results would be achieved by contextualising teaching within subject modules and as part of feedback. The different perspectives and contacts we could contribute were valuable here in mediating the toolkit materials to teaching staff.

Drawing on our collective bank of experiences and particular professional expertise gave authority to our promotion of the materials and made it possible to produce examples for usage that were relevant to a variety of teaching situations. It also prompted thoughts about future co-teaching initiatives, particularly between library and learning development teams.

Finally we noted a lack of awareness in students about the need to develop their referencing practices to suit higher-level studies and more complex communications when moving up to university (or to postgraduate study). Students felt they did not need to learn about referencing because they had successfully used it at school or college, or in their previous studies overseas (in both cases, usually a more basic version than is needed at university). The notion of referencing as a finite and bordered standalone skill exacerbated this belief. In addition, students had a narrow mental definition of plagiarism that limited it to deliberate acts of cheating.

This also discouraged engagement, fostering a belief that plagiarism was not something that they needed to worry about. Academics' emphasis on avoiding plagiarism became defined as a negative activity undertaken to avoid punishment rather than to develop and enhance academic writing. The notion of 'academic integrity' suggested a solution to this problem, offering a positive, aspirational and developmental model within which referencing could be situated.

As an overarching concept that embraced both information and academic literacy practices as well as recognising the distinct character of different academic disciplines, it also allowed us to find a space that readily accommodated our collective expertise.

Extending our collaborative reach

A significant advantage of bringing together representatives from diverse professions was that we all had our own professional networks (local and national) that we could draw on to support our investigations. The national networks were especially helpful in the early part of our research when we sought to understand the broader picture of responses to student referencing issues at other institutions.

Postings on a number of professional mailing lists elicited a range of fruitful responses, considering the issues from a variety of angles. We learnt that identifying the overlaps between professions and participating in each other's networks can offer a different viewpoint on support issues and promote creative solutions. In addition, a single researcher, working from the perspective of one professional field, would have struggled to identify and collect such a spread of information in such a short time.

While the diversity of expertise and experiences we were able to access was creatively advantageous, it was important that we found a way to control the mass of inputs we accumulated by identifying a concept that embraced all of our interests and concerns. A strong theme that emerged from this early information-gathering reinforced our movement away from a narrow focus on avoiding plagiarism and towards the more positive conception of 'academic integrity' (Morris, 2010).Through our contacts we were able to identify a number of institutions that were already using this notion with students, and collected first-hand accounts from staff of their development processes and how they were working in practice. Academic integrity became a central tenet of our resource development but little had yet appeared in the academic journals that we had expected to be the main focus of our secondary research because use of the concept in UK institutions was relatively recent.

Without our diverse networks it would have been far less easy to identify as a trend and gain an overview of its use.

In addition to productive external networking, team members were also able to draw on diverse groups of contacts within the University, in both academic departments and support services. Educational research projects can succeed or fail on the ability to attract a suitable range of participants. Having team members working in three different sectors in the University multiplied the number of people with whom we had already developed working relationships. This helped considerably in engaging them with the project, and in their willingness to disseminate information about our research to others, both staff and students. We were also able to utilise our internal communities of practice to raise awareness of the project and collect data from whole groups.

These included liaison librarians, language tutors, and teaching and learning communities. In these networks, even if individuals had not already established working relationships with team members, the fact that they were co-members of a network made it easier both to frame questions so that they were relevant to the group (for instance, by utilising common examples), and to gather responses (for instance, by being able to credibly show how the research would benefit them in their working practices).

Members of these networks extended our potential reach further. For instance, each academic department has a named liaison librarian and a nominated library rep from the academic tutors, so discussions with the liaison librarian network could be progressed into the academic departments. Teaching and learning communities included the School Directors of Teaching and Learning and University Teaching Fellows, giving us access to senior figures with an interest in supporting and promoting independent learning.

As a result of these scaffolded networking strategies, we were able to access and engage a considerable portion of local stakeholders through a distributed use of time amongst team members.

However, perhaps our greatest success in engaging an internal network came when we sent out a survey via email to students. Being aware that bulk emails are often ignored, and that a certain amount of survey fatigue was setting in among the student population anyway, we decided to recruit administrative staff in departments to promote the survey directly to their students. The survey took place just before Easter, so we had determined that we would offer a prize draw for participants with chocolate eggs as prizes. Our research officer had the excellent idea of offering an additional prize to the administrative staff member who had forwarded the original email to the top prize-winning student. The survey was very widely promoted and had a high rate of responses in a short period of time, and we had the great pleasure of making one member of department administrative staff (often not sufficiently recognised for the support they give to students) very happy.

Developing the Toolkit

In keeping with the various perspectives that each team member had brought to the project and the key messages gained from our research, we took a holistic approach to the contents of the toolkit. The familiar formatting examples were included alongside advice on using references to give authority to academic writing, how to find bibliographic details and understand reading lists, interpreting *Turnitin* originality reports, and a glossary of terms associated with referencing that are frequently used in academia. Referring back to the need to make materials adaptable to different contexts, all documents were made available in printed and digital formats with handouts and exercise sheets kept to one or two sides of A4 to avoid guidance fatigue. Particular attention was paid to images, layout and readability to promote engagement. To encourage tutors to use the materials as embedded study skills teaching situated within their subject modules, we included discrete PowerPoint slides on aspects of referencing and avoiding plagiarism that could be added to subject teaching. We also produced brief animated video tutorials that could be promoted to students as engaging self-access resources to reinforce teaching in the classroom. Links were made to relevant guidance from both the Library and Study Advice to draw out the particular areas of expertise of each team, for instance, guidance on finding bibliographic details and using referencing management programs from the Library, and on the role of referencing in academic writing and other supporting practices like note making and time management from the Study Advice team. While the Toolkit itself was designed for teaching and self-access purposes, links to external material extended our communications to students about when they might contact each service for further advice. Throughout this process, our diverse expertise and experience produced a broadly contextualised interpretation of the research that informed the development of more effective and engaging support for student success.

With team members using writing in their professional roles in very different ways and for different purposes, there was a danger that the outcomes of the project which involved large amounts of writing (the toolkit, guide and various reports) might have read as fragmented texts with a variety of voices. This was demonstrated in our first interim report produced for the funding panel, for which we used a writing process whereby the overall structure and outline was discussed and agreed by the team with team members nominated to write individual sections. It was noted by members of the panel that the different voices were clearly discernible. Given that the funding panel were aware of the diverse professional backgrounds of team members, it was a concern that this could have had an impact on the way the sections were read and prioritised. In the case of the student-facing resources, contrasting voices might have produced the impression of the very inconsistency we were trying to overcome.

To avoid this fragmentation in writing, we adopted a process in which a single team member wrote first drafts of each text (handouts, exercises and answers, report sections). This was then posted on the wiki for team members to given feedback and suggest revisions.

The original author would then edit the text, with a single editor doing a final edit to maintain the single voice. Although this could mean a disproportionate amount of editing work was carried out by one person, it was also easier to write drafts knowing that they would be evaluated and refined by the rest of the team. The overall result was the achievement of a coherent and consistent feel to the toolkit materials.

Lessons for future collaborations

Being a part of the *'What did I do wrong?'* project gave us the opportunity to gain a number of insights into processes that facilitate successful collaboration between individuals from different professional backgrounds. Some of these were anticipated and planned for (for instance, the communications strategy, creative brainstorming at our face-to-face meetings), but others emerged as part of the process (the immense value of distributed networking, the coherence produced by utilising a single authorial voice). With each team member acting as an 'insider' in the sense of being involved in supporting students, who was able to take an 'outsider' view of other members' contributions, the outcomes were much greater than the sum of their parts, but this could not have happened so successfully without the swift development of trust between team members (Bailey, 2010; Dennis and Robert, 2009). These are lessons that we have drawn from this experience and will apply to the continuing development of library/learning development collaboration in the future. Already we have used our experience and understanding of each other's roles to promote and increase the amount of co-teaching involving Liaison Librarians and Study Advisers, and our respective student-facing guidance materials on referencing have been drawn together in a single joint online guide. In addition, we are able to offer a more integrated response to wider University activities such as open days, enhancement and induction programmes.

Perhaps the most crucial lesson was the importance of mutual respect and equality of value for different professional roles. The traditional hierarchies that value university staff employed on academic contracts above those employed in other professional roles overlook the potential for the university as a *de facto* community of practice. In Wenger (1998, pp.73-82) this is defined as a group of individuals that share "mutual engagement…joint enterprise…shared repertoire".

In the case of the university, these are aligned with the venture we are all involved in: enabling the creation and sharing of knowledge. While our different professional roles link us to more diverse local networks and professional communities, this single shared purpose recognises the equal value of all contributors to a common end. Current economic cutbacks and threats of outsourcing may encourage a tendency to retreat into defensive silos, but we need to recognise that collaborations that act on this mutual professional understanding and respect for one another's roles hold the potential to produce great and long-lasting benefits for all students and university staff.

References

Andretta, S. 2005. *Information literacy: A practitioner's guide*. Oxford: Chandos Publishing.

Appleton, L. 2005. Examination of the impact of information-skills training on the academic work of health studies students: a single case study. *Health Information and Libraries Journal*. 22(3), pp.164-172.

Bailey, R. 2010. The role and efficacy of generic learning and study support: what is the experience and perspective of academic teaching staff? *Journal of Learning Development in Higher Education* 2. [Online]. [Accessed 27 November 2014]. Available from http://www.aldinhe.ac.uk/ojs/index.php?journal=jldhe&page=article&op=view&path[]=57.

Becher, T. and Trowler, P.R. 2001. *Academic tribes and territories.* 2nd ed. Buckingham: Society for Research into Higher Education.

Belzowski, N.F. et al. 2013. Crafting identity, collaboration, and relevance for academic librarians using communities of practice. *Collaborative Librarianship.*-Online]. 5(1), pp.3-15. [Accessed 13 August 2014]. Available from http://collaborativelibrarianship.org/index.php/jocl/article/viewArticle/212.

Blythman, M. and Orr, S. 2002. A joined-up policy approach to student support. In: Peelo, M. and Wareham, T. eds. *Failing students in higher education*. Buckingham: Open University Press and The Society for Research in Higher Education, pp.45-55.

CILIP. 2013. *What is the professional knowledge and skills base?*. [Online]. [Accessed 13 August 2014]. Available from: http://www.cilip.org.uk/cilip/jobs-and-careers/professional-knowledge-and-skills-base/what-professional-knowledge-and-skills.

Cottrell, S. 2013. Revolution by stealth: the impact of learning development on democratising intelligence through constructive approaches to student support. *Journal of Learning Development in Higher Education*. **6**. [Online]. [Accessed 13 August 2014]. Available from: http://www.aldinhe.ac.uk/ojs/index.php?journal=jldhe&page=article&op=view&path[]=221.

Dennis, A. R. and Robert, L.P. 2009. Individual swift trust and knowledge-based trust in face-to-face and virtual team members. *Journal of Management Information Systems*. **26**(2), pp.241-279.

Durkin, K., & Main, A. 2002. Discipline-based study skills support for first-year undergraduate students. *Active Learning in Higher Education*. **3**(1), pp.24-39.

Hanson, T. ed. 2005. Managing academic support services in universities: the convergence experience. London: Facet Publishing

HEFCE. 2014. Global demand for UK higher education. Bristol: HEFCE.

Hilsdon, J. 2011. What is learning development? In: Hartley, P. et al. eds. *Learning development in Higher Education*. Basingstoke: Palgrave Macmillan, pp.13-27.

Melling, M. 2013. Collaborative service provision through super-convergence. In: Melling, M. and Weaver, M. eds. *Collaboration in libraries and learning environments*. London: Facet Publishing, pp.149-165.

Morris, E. 2010. *Supporting academic integrity: approaches and resources for higher education* The Higher Education Academy: JISC Academic Integrity Service. [Online]. [Accessed 27 November 2014]. Available from: http://www.heacademy.ac.uk/resources/detail/academicintegrity/Supporting_academic_integrity_approaches_and_resources_for_HE

Neville, C. 2010. *The Complete Guide to Referencing and Avoiding Plagiarism*. 2nd ed. Maidenhead: Open University Press.

Office of the Independent Adjudicator. 2013. *Annual Report*. Reading: Office of the Independent Adjudicator.

Roberts, S. 2005. New professional identities and practices for learner support. In: Levy, P. and Roberts, S. eds. *Developing the new learning environment*, London: Facet Publishing, pp.91-110.

Tennant, P. et al. 2007. Academic Misconduct Benchmarking Researching Project Part 1: The Range and Spread of Penalties available for student plagiarism among UK higher education institutions. JISC Plagiarism Advisory Service. [Online]. [Accessed 13 August 2014]. Available from: http://archive.plagiarismadvice.org/documents/amber/FinalReport.pdf.

Thomas, L. et al. 2005. From the margins to the mainstream: embedding widening participation in HE. London: Universities UK.

Walsh, L. 2010. Constructive Interference: Wikis And Service Learning In The Technical Communication Classroom. *Technical Communication Quarterly*. **19**(2), pp.184-211.

Wenger, E. 1998. *Communities of Practice: Learning, Meaning and Identity*. Cambridge: Cambridge University Press.

Whittaker, R. 2008. The First Year Experience: Transition to and During the First Year. Glasgow: QAA Scotland.

Transforming practice and promoting academic excellence through collaborative cross-unit partnerships

By Vicki Bourbous and Tina Bavaro

About the authors

Tina Bavaro BEd, MEd, EdD

Tina is a senior lecturer and academic developer at Australian Catholic University. She completed a doctoral degree from Virginia Polytechnic Institute and State University, USA where she majored in Curriculum and Instruction (in Higher Education) and Educational Technology. Her research focused on the implementation of new engineering curriculum that integrated innovative simulation technologies. She also obtained a Masters (with a major in Curriculum Studies and Research) and Bachelor of Education degree from the University of Sydney. Tina was offered her first lectureship by the University of Sydney. In 2004 she was the successful recipient of the NSW Minister's Quality Teaching Award. In 2007, with federal government funding she designed a personalised workplace continuing professional learning program for educators based on the concept of Educational Mentoring. Since 2012 until Semester 2, 2015 Tina has been the Lecturer-in-Charge of the foundations unit of the Graduate Certificate in Higher Education, UNHE500 Learning and Teaching in Higher Education and UNHE501 Curriculum, Assessment and Evaluation. During the past four and a half years UNHE500 enrolment numbers have grown exponentially. This unit has been benchmarked as best practice with the Office for Learning and Teaching Advancing Academic Professionalisation Project: National Benchmarking of Graduate Certificates for Higher Education.

Vicki Bourbous BEd (Hons), MIM, GCHE

Vicki Bourbous is the Liaison Librarian for the School of Education at Australian Catholic University. Her qualifications include degrees in Education, Information Management and Higher Education. Vicki was instrumental in developing an online pilot project which formed the foundation for an online information literacy program in 2012. This resulted in the formation of a project team and a successful grant application to further develop the online program. Apart from developments in information literacy and online learning, Vicki has an interest in the use of emerging technologies both for teaching and learning and also for collaboration and productivity, and has also presented at conferences and workshops on this topic.

Introduction

Expansion of online learning in higher education demands that every tertiary educator must be equipped to design and teach programs that are partially or fully online (Reeves and Reeves, 2012; Allen and Seaman, 2010). Together, professional staff from the University Library, Academic Skills Unit and the Academic Developer from the Learning and Teaching Centre (LTC) at Australia Catholic University embarked on a journey of collaboration to produce an information and academic literacy online resource for first year undergraduate students.

This chapter explains why an interprofessional collaboration was necessary for this project, and in particular why it was vital for the Library to collaborate and build strategic partnerships in order to maximise expertise from academic skills and learning and teaching partners, to minimise duplication by learning support units, and to share resources.

Building strategic partnerships to achieve a shared understanding aligned to the University's core values and policies was a gradual process, and not without its issues. Challenging the learning and teaching assumptions of partners took time as there were many diverse viewpoints that reflected individual experiences and expertise.

A design-based research (DBR) methodology will be presented as a possible framework to aid partnership working. Systematic DBR interventions were crucial in strengthening partner relationships, developing and obtaining feedback on the resource, transforming practice, and in ensuring partner and key stakeholder support.

While this collaborative project had a specific output; namely, the online resource; the long-term benefits to staff were of equal significance. This chapter will place a focus on how professional development opportunities were built into the project with the aim that this would lead to long-term transformative change for the librarians involved.

Why a collaborative approach?

The setting for this collaborative partnership was a large, publicly funded Catholic university in Australia with campuses located in Brisbane, Sydney (North Sydney and Strathfield), Canberra, Adelaide, Melbourne and Ballarat (see Figure 1 below). It has over 30,000 students (both undergraduate and postgraduate) and more than 1,800 staff.

Figure 1 Geographical location of the campuses.

As a result of this geographical spread, information and academic literacy skills had previously been addressed through a somewhat fragmented approach, leading to a duplication of effort as each campus designed and delivered its own programs. Learning support services like the Academic Skills Unit and the Library worked separately, unaligned to the undergraduate curriculum or graduate attributes. Due to expanding enrolments and the increasing diversity of the student cohort at all campuses, face-to-face instruction during lectures and tutorials was not deemed sustainable. By utilising the expertise and experiences of other learning support units, the Library initiated and led a project that aimed to provide a workable solution to these issues.

It was agreed early on that an online resource would provide an equitable 'open to everyone' approach to learning. It would provide a consistent mode of instruction across the seven campuses, allowing the Librarians to focus on designing high-quality learning activities and other content to integrate into the resource, rather than time-consuming face-to-face instruction that often resulted in passive experiences for the learner. In addition, all material would comply with accessibility requirements, and any student without a computer would be loaned a laptop or iPad, or would be able to complete the resource in the Library.

An interprofessional collaboration was essential for this project due to the range of skills sets and expertise required for the successful development of an online resource that came from across the different teams, including:

- research and information literacy skills for locating scholarly sources and evaluating information for the purposes of the assessment (liaison librarians, Library)
- academic integrity and referencing skills needed to use sourced information ethically (academic skills advisors, Academic Skills Unit)
- learning and instructional design for both online learning and professional development (PD) workshops to engage learners

and achieve the outcomes with an emphasis on student-centric curriculum (Academic Developer, Learning and Teaching Centre)

- technological skills to enhance the program and engage the students in learning using a variety of learning activities (Educational Technologist).

  The technologist was contracted in externally to bring technical expertise that would supplement internal knowledge and skills, and to provide a fresh approach to the design and creation of the online modules.

Figure 3 provides a visual representation of the layered partnerships both within the University's learning and teaching portfolio, and with the external support provided by the Educational Technologist.

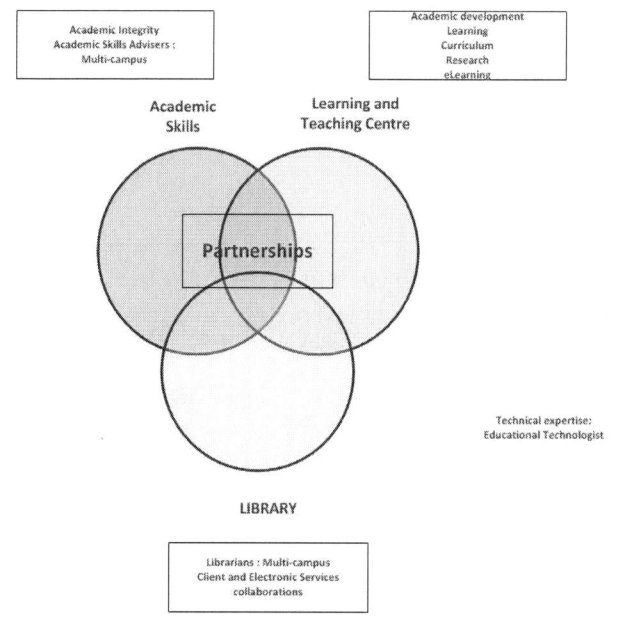

Figure 2. Layered partnerships at the University

The project team leader, a campus library manager, coordinated the collaborative partnerships between the units and campuses. Not only did she have the skills and experience in leadership and overseeing a number of previous projects but she had also lobbied for, and successfully piloted, the Library's first embedded online information literacy program in 2011.

The project team leader's people-oriented management and leadership style encouraged all parties to feel that their input was valued, and to take ownership of the project. She was also able to identify personal skills and attributes that could be used for the benefit of the project. For instance, apart from the specific expertise brought by each team, individual staff members displayed excellence in writing, editing, creating demonstration videos using screen capture software, and presenting and selling the project to academics.

The project team leader never lost sight of the big picture, ensuring that the vision, values and goals driving the collaboration were communicated effectively. The collaboration was very much underpinned by the University's student-centric mission and its Service Matters Framework, which consists of a set of principles outlining the University's commitment to excellent service delivery. One of the key findings identified by students and staff that emerged during the 12 months of research that went into the Framework was a need to "enhance cross-unit collaboration and communication". The framework clearly states that "to achieve service excellence we need to work together" and "collaborate to implement improvements".

The design and implementation of the online resource was a living expression of these principles, and they directed the partners to an agreed way of operating and a commitment to working together. Of particular relevance to the project were the principles of:

- Collaboration: a commitment to working better together
- Quality: demonstrated through consistency, responsiveness and timeliness

- Adaptability: a systematic continuous improvement process applied to design and implement service changes
- Accountability: clarity of roles and responsibilities for outcomes
- Accessibility: services are available where and when they are needed
- Efficiency: streamlined processes and performance measurement

(Australian Catholic University, 2014)

All partners were personally responsible and accountable for adhering to and demonstrating the service principles through their work at the University. Respect for the dignity of the individual and the desire to build a community of practice influenced the way the collaborative partnerships between academic and professional staff developed in order to support the transformation of practice.

A framework for collaborative working

A design-based research (DBR) methodology was proposed by the Academic Developer (a researcher with doctoral qualifications from the Learning and Teaching Centre) to support partner collaborations. For the purpose of this chapter, design-based research is defined as:

"a *systematic* but flexible methodology aimed to improve educational practices through *iterative analysis, design, development and implementation* based on collaboration among the researchers and practitioners in real world settings" (Wang and Hannafin, 2005, p.6).

The literature on design-based research (Van den Akker, 1999; Reeves, Herrington and Oliver, 2005, Wang and Hannafin, 2005) proposes strategies for analysis, design, development and implementation that were useful in initiating and facilitating partner collaborations. DBR also ensured that partners and stakeholders such as undergraduate students and faculty academics were actively engaged in ongoing communication, consultation, professional development and iterative feedback. The DBR-informed methodology used in the project was applicable because it was interactive, flexible, aimed to work with an authentic problem through testing and interventions (Design-Based Research Collective, 2003; Van den Akker and et al., in press), and could be designed to work with key stakeholders in a university setting (Wang and Hannafin, 2005).

```
[ANALYSIS]    [DEVELOPMENT]         [TESTING]           [REFLECTION]
              Development of a      Iterative cycles of
              solution: The         testing
              innovation
                         ←———— Refinement of the resource ————↓
```

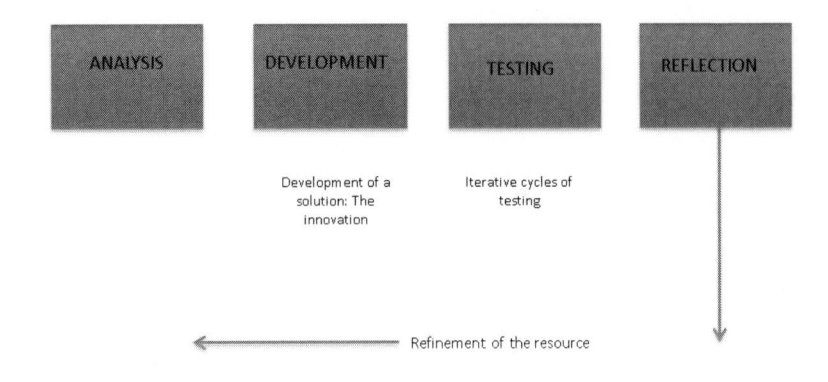

Figure 3 Phases of Design-based Research

The first phase involved collaborative **analysis** of the problem by the researcher (the Academic Developer) and the partners. The problem was the undergraduate students' research capacity, as identified through the frustration experienced by many academics with the quality of their students' outputs. Furthermore, enrolments at the University had significantly increased as a consequence of government initiatives to widen student participation in Australia (Bradley, 2008). All partners agreed that due to the increasing number of students that needed to develop research and academic skills, and be aware of support services and resources available to them, a move away from face-to-face delivery of instruction was required.

The second phase saw the **development** of the online resource, with a particular focus on equipping the large and diverse student population with the graduate attributes to "locate, organise, synthesise and evaluate information" (Australian Catholic University, 2009).

The goal was to create flexible, portable and user-focused tutorials using a range of web-based technologies to motivate and engage students from a range of educational backgrounds (Gunn et al., 2011).

The online resource consisted of five modules. The first three aimed to develop students' information literacy skills, including engaging them in using discipline-specific databases to obtain relevant scholarly information. The other two modules focused on University policies and frameworks relevant to academic integrity, as well as the academic skills related to this area such as writing and referencing. Integrated throughout the resource were formative quizzes to provide immediate feedback and reinforcement of what had been learnt. Badging in the form of a certificate of achievement was generated on successful completion of the graded quizzes. After supplying a concept brief, the Educational Technologist developed the interactive resources to be integrated into the University's learning management system.

Iterative cycles of **testing** and evaluation interventions were carried out, including a train-the-trainer professional development (PD) program, a showcase face-to-face workshop for academic staff and Library staff not involved in the development of the resource, formative feedback from students through online surveys, and professional development of faculty academics through the Graduate Certificate in Higher Education workshops. These interventions helped to support a fundamental change in perspective regarding the online resource, as will be explored later in the chapter.

The final phase was one of **reflection**. Data collected during the testing and evaluation was used to improve the educational experience for the student. Evaluation data from students included feedback on the user interface, navigation, and appropriateness of the modules, learning activities, and both the formative summative assessments. This afforded an opportunity for the partners to rethink elements of the design and content in order to improve the initial prototype, and changes were made to the resource based on this feedback and evaluation.

The DBR cycle was then repeated at the end of 2013 to inform further updates and amendments to the resource for the 2014 version. As a result of this engagement, students became evaluators, quality controllers, and future advocates for the online modules.

Benefits of the collaborative approach

Firstly, the collaboration benefitted the students. The online resource provided a consistent mode of instruction across the seven campuses, and students could now access content produced by different experts in one place. To illustrate, the collaboration between the Librarian and Academic Skills advisor on the academic integrity sections ensured that the content included information on both writing and referencing. This included working together to provide exemplars on how to edit a written assignment to produce a high quality final product, covering effective paraphrasing, the development of arguments and accurate referencing. Bringing the two professions together ensured that the students were presented with a holistic view of the concept of academic integrity, rather than addressing referencing and writing as two separate processes.

STEP 2: Here's Benson's first draft of a paragraph. He's using the APA referencing system for his assignments (you may be asked to use another style in your units). He's got some problems with his referencing and use of evidence. Can you identify what they are?

Review of Benson's first draft (image) or as text.

STEP 3: After talking with an Academic Skills Adviser, Benson did a bit more work on his paragraph. It's still not there yet, though.

Have a look at the comments to see what he still needs to work on.

Review of Benson's second draft (image) or as text.

STEP 4: Here's Benson's final draft. He's integrated information from his sources well, appropriately cited it, and structured the paragraph in a clear way.

Review of Benson's final draft (image) or as text.

Figure 4: Modelling good academic writing

Another clear benefit of the collaborative approach was the increased exposure that it afforded the project: partnership between the learning support units and faculty academics helped to get the online resource embedded into the undergraduate curriculum.

This was deemed as key to its success as numerous studies have shown that embedding literacies within the curriculum is of benefit to the learner (Price, Becker, Clarke and Collins, 2011, Gunn, Hearne and Sibthorpe, 2011).

To illustrate, the Learning and Teaching Centre realized the value of the online resource as a professional development opportunity for academic staff. The Academic Developer was also the lecturer in charge of the foundations unit, and the course coordinator of the Graduate Certificate in Higher Education (GCHE).

The online modules were embedded into the GCHE professional development course for teaching staff at the University. This involved mandating the modules as an assessment task within the first unit of the course; participants were required to complete the modules and submit a certificate of achievement. Although some academics resented this as they considered the task time consuming, the strategy nevertheless provided a catalyst for early adopter academics to embed the online modules into their courses for first year students. The outcome of this cross-unit collaboration assisted faculty academics in addressing a range of graduate attributes within their course assessments.

Transforming practice

Interprofessional collaborations have the potential to initiate long-term change in practice, both for the partners involved and for others within the institution. While the primary aim of the collaboration was to produce an online resource for students, a number of interventions were built in throughout the project to prompt a substantial change in the way that the librarians viewed learning and teaching, and ultimately to change their way of working. This ensured that the collaboration was not just about the immediate project but also a significant long-term change in practice.

Merizow's (1991) transformative dimensions of adult learning is a useful lens through which we can observe the experience of the partners involved in the collaboration.

The dimensions that Merizow outlines include experiencing a dilemma, self-examination of practice, critical self-reflection of practice, exploring new ideas, and acquiring new knowledge and skills for implementing a new course of action.

In the first instance, the librarians experienced the dilemma of an expanding and diverse cohort and an outdated mode of instruction. Furthermore, after consultation with faculty academics, there was a concern that undergraduate students' research capacity and academic writing skills were lacking, as corroborated by the literature (Price,

Becker, Clark, and Collins, 2011; Salisbury and Sheridan, 2011; Wade, Locke, and Devey, 2012). They then self-examined their current professional practice. A critical self-reflection based on the alignment of their role as liaison librarians and their teaching of information literacy led to individual assessments of their own assumptions regarding didactic face-to-face instructional practice. They realised that they would be unable to provide the required level of active face-to-face learning sessions within the curriculum for all students across all campuses. In order to tackle this issue, it was agreed that interactive and learner-centred online activities were required to engage and reach all students. The liaison librarians would need to work with their representative schools to embed the online modules within core first year units. It was at this stage that the librarians realised that they needed to up-skill in terms of online curriculum design, delivery and assessment. Acquiring new knowledge and skills for implementing the online resource would require professional development.

Interprofessional collaboration was essential to this upskilling. Librarians worked with colleagues from the Learning and Teaching Centre to develop a learning design for the online modules.

Designing online learning is a crucial curriculum challenge facing higher education educators. While learning design is often implicit, practice-based and content-focussed, Oliver and Herrington's model (2001) was employed to useful effect here as it offered a visual representation of the learning that was expected to occur during the user's interaction with the online modules.

The model includes three elements:

- **Learning tasks/activities**: comprising the context, processes and conditions by which the learner is engaged so as to digest information, practise, apply and reflect. These represent tasks and activities to be undertaken by the student. When designing the online resource, the team designed the tasks and activities to

ensure the intended skills and attributes could be achieved by the students.
- **Resources**: including the materials such as the information the student needs to acquire.
- **Support:** including the strategies and processes that assist the student to work beyond their comfort zone.

The Academic Developer added an extra element to the model that represents formative assessment for learning (such as feedback to enhance learning), and summative assessment of learning (such as a grade or in this case, a certificate of achievement).

This way of thinking about learning and teaching was new to many of the librarians. Whereas before their teaching was didactic, focusing on telling students what they needed to know in a face-to-face environment, this new approach as introduced by the Academic Developer provided students with the opportunity to actively engage in learning tasks, receive feedback and therefore be able to test their own understanding of the material being delivered.

Professional development opportunities

It was not just the librarians that were involved in the collaborative project who benefitted from the opportunity to upskill and reflect on their practice. Fundamental to the success of this project was the engagement of all of the liaison librarians, as they would be instrumental in promoting the resource to academic staff and students as well as in considering how the resource could be used in teaching. Moreover, to make the most of the collaboration it was important to consider how long-term change of professional practice could be ensured. Transforming the work practices of the librarians involved a train-the-trainer-style approach to professional development.

The showcase workshop

One way this was achieved was through a professional development showcase workshop. The librarians working on the project collaborated with the Academic Developer to design a workshop for other librarians, academic skills advisors and faculty academic staff.

The aims of the workshop were for the attendees to:

- contribute ideas and expertise to further develop the online resource
- explore and experience some of the learning activities from the online resource
- engage with local campus service support staff and develop an action plan for the implementation
- meet and discuss the resource with staff from various faculties and units
- reflect on how the online resource could be used in different teaching contexts

The showcase enabled the experienced librarians that were involved in the project to demonstrate the online resource to their less-experienced colleagues and those not involved directly in the development.

The workshop participants completed the online resource for themselves and practised teaching the modules to colleagues while providing valuable feedback to the project team. Also modelled at the workshop was a toolkit containing guides to help teach the modules and suggestions on how to conduct workshop sessions with faculty academics. Academics were invited to provide feedback on the prototype resource. Finally, librarians and other key stakeholders explored ideas of how they could implement and promote the online resource, and contribute strategically to ensuring the resource was a success on their respective campuses.

The workshop helped to give all relevant staff a sense of ownership, and to build a pool of competent librarians to support the implementation of the online resource. For the librarians specifically, the workshop enabled them to:

- engage in discussion and participate in a forum
- think, pair and share an action-based scenario of how they would implement the online resource on their campus and what resources and time would be needed to achieve this
- have a follow-up final discussion and reflection on various learnings and concerns to clarify issues and to support each other
- take away a toolkit to support the implementation and adoption of the online resource on their respective campuses and by their school academics.

Teaching qualification

Librarians were also given the opportunity to complete the Graduate Certificate in Higher Education taught by the Academic Developer as part of their professional development. Some librarians had already completed the course and had a strong foundation for implementing online curricula based on contemporary research into student learning. The more experienced librarians were then able to support their less experienced colleagues in acquiring the new knowledge and skills needed for implementing this new online resource.

Mentoring

Another opportunity that the librarians could participate in was educational mentoring: personalised, developmental professional development within the context of their work environment and practice, which was offered by the Academic Developer (Bavaro, 2015).

Educational mentoring involves making ongoing educational improvements over an extended time frame with a capable peer (i.e. an educational mentor) in a supportive environment. The interactions, ongoing complex conversations and critical self-reflections help build mentee's self-esteem, morale and confidence as well as extending knowledge and skills.

During this project the Academic Developer became a critical friend to librarian colleagues and served as a catalyst or change agent for the transformation of instructional practice. This one-on-one collaborative relationship contributed to the development of a trusted and collegial partnership between the Library professional staff and the Academic Developer.

The Academic Developer also assisted the librarians in writing and submitting a grant application, providing support, advice and constructive feedback. Senior staff supported the successful application, which provided University funds in the form of a teaching development grant to develop the online resource and deliver a professional development program.

Long-term impact on librarians' practice

Perhaps the greatest change for the librarians as a result of this collaboration was a refocus on promoting academic excellence and liaising more closely with academic staff. This began with discussions between librarians and academics on how to implement the online resource into core first year modules, and has continued with ongoing discussions about how the Library can support academic staff in further developing information literate students. Following this project, it was decided that there would be a Single Service Point (SSP) model across campuses to streamline services. Rather than liaison librarians staffing these as previously been the case, they are now staffed by upskilled paraprofessionals who support students with their basic information enquiries, leaving the librarians with more time to focus on their academic liaison role.

Liaison librarians now have the skills to develop online resources and the confidence to collaborate with academic staff and other learning support services on various initiatives and projects. Now that first year instruction is provided mainly through the online resource, librarians are now focusing on more advanced instruction for the later years, postgraduates and researchers. Furthermore, communicating, promoting and embedding services within faculties is now a core function of the librarians' work.

Finally, now that librarians have the foundation and collaborative relationships to build upon, they are being invited to join other projects that require input from learning support services. For example, an Advisory Group was formed on building literacy assessment rubrics, and a librarian was asked to contribute to the group alongside academic skills advisors and academic staff. This would not have happened before the collaboration, and the fostering of relationships with other professionals in the University that the project enabled.

Conclusion

Information and academic literacy are clearly important 'rules of the game' for first year students to learn and succeed at university. Through an interprofessional collaboration involving staff from the Library, Academic Skills Unit and the Learning and Teaching Centre, an online module was successfully developed, deployed and embedded in the curriculum for all new first year students, giving them a consistent mode of instruction and a chance to engage actively in their own learning through interactive learning activities and formative and summative assessment.

This interprofessional and cross-campus collaboration not only achieved the immediate goal of providing this new learning experience to first years but, through the collaborative partnerships that were formed, learning support colleagues, (the librarians in particular) were challenged to re-think their perceptions about learning and to change how the literacy graduate attribute to be able to "locate, organise, analyse, synthesise and evaluate information" should be taught and assessed.

This joint venture transformed work and instructional practice to enhance student learning and promote academic excellence at the University. Professional development events were crucial in empowering all of the liaison librarians to transform their teaching practices.

This collaboration became more than just working together to produce an online resource. The inclusion of the professional development opportunities meant that the librarians in particular were able to develop skills in a number of areas including delivering online learning, writing grant applications and implementing cross-University initiatives to make long-term changes to the way information literacy skills in particular are taught at the University.

The authors hope that by sharing their experience and efforts, other university libraries will consider the potential of interprofessional collaborations with other learning support units. It is important that libraries build and utilise partnerships to promote student success and academic excellence, but also that opportunities to develop skills and professional practice is built into these collaborative endeavours.

References

Australian Catholic University. 2014. *The service matters framework: a strategy for delivery at ACU*. [Online]. [Accessed 26 October 2015]. Available from: https://www.acu.edu.au/__data/assets/pdf_file/0011/726077/Service_Matters.pdf

Allen, E andSeaman, J.2010. *Class differences: online education in the United States*. The Sloan Consortium, Needham: MA.

Andrews, T., and Patil, R. 2007. Information Literacy for first-year students: An embedded curriculum approach. *European Journal of Engineering Education*, 32(3), pp.253-259.

Bradley, D., Noonan, P., Nugent, H. and Scales, B. 2008. *Review of Australian Higher Education: Final Report*. [Online]. [Accessed 26 October 2015].Available from: http://www.voced.edu.au/content/ngv32134

Gunn, C., Hearne, S., and Sibthorpe, J. 2011. Right from the start: A rationale for embedding academic literacy skills in university courses. *Journal of University Teaching & Learning Practice*. [Online]. 8(1), 1-10. [Accessed 26 October 2015]. Available from: http://ro.uow.edu.au/jutlp/vol8/iss1/6/

Gurney, L. J., and Wilkes, J. 2008. Creating a library presence in online units. *Australian Academic & Research Libraries*, 39(1), 26-37.

Mezirow, J.1991. *Transformative dimensions of adult learning*. San Francisco: Jossey Bass.

Oliver, R., and Herrington, J. 2001. *Teaching and learning online: A beginner's guide to e-learning and e-teaching in higher education.* [Online]. [Date accessed 26 October 2015]. Available from: http://elrond.scam.ecu.edu.au/oliver/2002/TALO2.pdf

Porter, J. A., Wolbach, K. C., Purzycki, C. B., Bowman, L. A., Agbada, E., and Mostrom, A. M. 2010. Integration of information and scientific literacy: Promoting literacy in undergraduates. *CBE Life Sci Educ*, 9(4), pp.536-542.

Price, R., Becker, K., Clark, L., & Collins, S. 2011. Embedding information literacy in a first-year business undergraduate course. *Studies in Higher Education*, 36(6), pp.705-718.

Reeves, T.C and Reeves, P.M. 2012. Designing online and blended learning. In: Hunt, L and Chalmers, D. eds., *University teaching in focus: a learning–centred approach*. Melbourne: ACER Press,pp.112-127.

Salisbury, F., and Sheridan, L. 2011. Mapping the journey: developing an information literacy strategy as part of curriculum reform. *Journal of Librarianship and Information Science*. 43(3), pp.185-193.

Wade, A., Locke, J., and Devey, P. 2012. *An online information literacy course for undergraduates: early experiences*. IFLA World Library and Information Congress: 78th IFLA General Conference and Assembly, 11-17 August 2012, Helsinki, Finland. Available from: http://conference.ifla.org/past-wlic/2012/93-wade-en.pdf

Living, learning, and the Library: A collaborative effort to bring information literacy, research, and beyond classroom experiences to residence halls

By Ngoc-Yen Tran and Elizabeth Cantor

About the authors

Ngoc-Yen Tran, Outreach & Student Engagement Librarian, University Libraries, University of Oregon.

Yen is the Outreach & Student Engagement Librarian at the University of Oregon. She received her Master in Library and Information Science from the University of Washington's iSchool and her bachelor's degrees in English and art history from Willamette University. Yen's job is multifaceted, including creatively managing a small residence hall library called the Global Scholars Hall Library Commons, building and sustaining campus partnerships, working with international studies department students and faculty, and developing opportunities that engage students with the UO Libraries and librarians. When she is not at work, she is crafting or out on a hike.

Elizabeth Cantor, Coordinator of Instructional Support in Languages and Writing, Multicultural Center for Academic Excellence, University of Minnesota.

Lizzy earned her bachelor's degrees in psychology and criminal justice from George Washington University and her master's degree in Higher Education Student Affairs from the University of South Carolina. Most of her professional background is in Residence Life where she was responsible for managing a residence hall and forming relationships with academic partners. She now coordinates instructional support in writing for an office that serves traditionally underrepresented students at the

University of Minnesota. In her spare time, Lizzy loves being active and spending time outside.

Introduction

Much learning in higher education happens outside of the classroom. In this chapter, we discuss an innovative collaboration at the University of Oregon (UO) between University Housing and Residence Life and the University Libraries to bring living, learning and library experiences to students housed in a newly-built residence hall. We offer an initial overview of the foundation of Residence Life and living-learning communities to contextualize the initiative and then, using Kezar's 2001 study on establishing effective collaborations in higher education as an analytical framework, we examine how the collaboration was formed and sustained over time, and how we addressed challenges. This chapter offers practical insights, methodologies and best practices on how to work collaboratively with other departments on campus, built on a shared philosophy that focuses on the importance of student learning.

Drivers for collaboration

Kezar's 2001 article reviewed the results of a national study on the types of collaborations between academic and student affairs to draw out best practices for successful partnerships. She states that there are four main reasons for collaborations between student and academic affairs on college campuses: focus on student learning, environmental, managerial/accountability, and leadership. Kezar notes that, because many partnerships promote student learning, it is important to distinguish whether this is indeed the driving impetus for the partnership in the first place or if other motivations are in fact primary. Environmental partnerships refer to the campus ethos and whether or not the campus encourages collaborations between different departments. Managerial partnerships often stem from a source external to the partnering organizations such as legislatures, accreditors, or administrators. Finally, collaborations based on leadership refer to partnerships that are suggested by those with power on campus.

Kezar's study found that collaborations with a shared philosophical focus on student learning were found to be slightly more successful in creating effective partnerships.

We use this framework to analyse the drivers shaping our initiative to better understand the reasons behind the challenges we experienced and the successes we achieved.

The partnership between University Housing and the UO Libraries in the new residence hall on the UO campus was founded on a shared philosophy focused on student learning. However, as the development of the residence hall progressed and multiple other stakeholders became involved in the project, the shared philosophy got lost among other reasons for collaboration, namely managerial directions and leadership philosophies. Because we were charged by the administration with ensuring that the initial goals of the residence hall were realized, we took ownership and reframed the collaboration by focusing on the original shared philosophy: to put student learning at the forefront of our work. This chapter demonstrates how this shared philosophy helped us to develop a successful collaboration.

Beyond the classroom learning

University Housing and Residence Life

As professionals who believe that learning can and should take place beyond the classroom, higher education theorists and student affairs practitioners have focused on a number of 'high impact' practices that increase student engagement and success on college campuses (Kuh, 2008). Student engagement is defined as the time that students are spending both on their coursework and on "other educationally purposeful activities" (National Survey of Student Engagement [NSSE], 2014). Universities and colleges can increase the amount of time students are likely to spend on these activities by ensuring that they are offered in a number of iterations across the student experience (NSSE, 2014). These practices include first-year seminars, common intellectual experiences (such as common reading), learning communities, writing-intensive courses, collaborative assignments and projects, undergraduate research, diversity/global learning, service learning, internships, and capstone courses and projects (Kuh, 2008).

With regard to residence life practices, research has consistently supported the view that living on campus assists students in developing stronger social skills, a tie to the institution, increased opportunities for interaction with faculty and, at times, positive academic involvement (Pascarella and Terenzini, 2005). This residential experience can be and often is combined with some of the high impact practices listed above, such as collaborative learning and learning communities, in order to support student academic success outside of the classroom.

UO Libraries and information literacy

Information literacy is a necessity in our information-rich world. Information literacy is defined as "the set of integrated abilities encompassing the reflective discovery of information, the understanding of how information is produced and valued, and the use of information in creating new knowledge and participating ethically in communities of learning" (Association of College & Research Libraries [ACRL], 2015). Librarians' relationships with faculty and academic departments have been a traditional source of information literacy opportunities, with librarians acting as guest lecturers for courses within the departments with which they collaborate. However, in recent years, libraries have understood that there are a number of students that they are not reaching: those they may never see in a course (Kraemer, et al, 2003). Therefore, libraries and librarians are developing more creative strategies and outreach programs that allow them to reach out to students beyond the classroom. These efforts have included being in non-traditional digital and physical spaces such as text-messaging and student union buildings.

At UO, the focus of student affairs practitioners on high impact practices such as those mentioned above offers opportunities for collaborations between Residence Life and the Libraries.

One such collaboration is the designation of a library space within a residence hall focused on the living-learning experience, which encourages learning and student academic success inside and outside of the classroom context.

Introducing the collaboration

In the planning stages of a new residence hall that was to be built on campus, University Housing and Residence Life and the University Libraries decided to embark on a significant collaborative initiative to provide beyond-the-classroom learning to students. The plan was to include a library that would bring more learning opportunities to student living spaces. For a long time, UO Libraries had worked with University Housing and Residence Life on a number of small projects and initiatives. In 2009, the UO had plans to build a new residence hall on the main campus that would include classrooms and a number of academic programs. In order to further the student academic experience and to promote student learning in the new residence hall on the dense residential side of campus, the library was brought into the conversation for all of the reasons that Kezar mentioned in the study: the campus culture encouraged including a variety of partners in order to grow the academic philosophies for the new building, and, new leadership and external partners also pushed for library involvement. Through discussions it was decided that the space located prominently on the first floor would be designated as a library equipped with a classroom, group study rooms, technology, a small book collection and a full-time librarian to manage it.

As a collaborative learning space, it was expected that the librarian, a professional Residence Life staff member, and the resident scholar (live-in faculty) would work together to support the academic programs in the building, the residents and anyone using the spaces in the building. In addition, it was expected that the librarian and Residence Life coordinator would work as a collaborative team in staff orientations and training, and to plan, organize and execute special events and programs with stakeholders (especially those involved with the building's academic programs). For Residence Life, having a library in the hall furthered their goals of integrating academic and living spaces. For the Libraries, there were opportunities to bring greater awareness of library resources, services and research opportunities to students, student staff and professional staff.

As well as deciding on the initial logistical details when we took up our new positions in 2012, we also had to make decisions about the space and how the collaborative relationship was going to move forward, keeping a focus on how these decisions would impact student learning. This project and our collaborative efforts will be the backdrop for discussing how we built, developed and sustained a collaboration between these two departments. At the start of each section hereafter, we outline our key transferrable lessons of how to make interprofessional collaborations work; we then go on to discuss how we applied each of these messages within our own context.

Developing the collaboration

- Agree what each party will contribute and document these decisions into a Memorandum of Understanding (MOU) as a source of referral.
- Engage in discussion about departmental goals and vision in order to determine opportunities for collaboration or improvements.
- Develop programmatic initiatives that will meet both collaborators' goals.

By the time we arrived in 2012, most of the decisions regarding objectives, staffing and operations of the shared space had already been made. A formal Memorandum of Understanding (MOU) created and signed by higher-level administration outlined what each party had agreed to contribute to the collaboration. The MOU included a section about the purpose and vision of the collaboration, as well as administrative details of who was responsible for staffing, management, technologies and security. It was agreed that University Housing would provide the space, as well as any facilities support the space might need. The Libraries, in turn, would hire a full-time librarian who would oversee all aspects of the space, including developing a library collection, providing support for the technologies, managing group study rooms and the seminar classroom and providing reference and research services to students. Books and other library materials, student and librarian wages and all technologies would be funded by the Libraries. The librarian would also be the main point of contact between the various parties in the hall.

Although the MOU was managerially driven and meant as a document for accountability and decision-making, its creation is based around student learning. We used the MOU whenever questions arose, or when we needed to reflect on the original purpose of the collaboration. For example, early on we had a question from all of the stakeholders about who could use the seminar classroom located in the library space. The MOU helped to establish ownership of the classroom and as a result, the Library developed guidelines for appropriate use. Additionally, when questions arose about facilities-related issues such as noise in the space, the team could look to the MOU to ensure we were responding within our roles. With the MOU, conflicts about responsibilities and ownership were alleviated, especially when all of the stakeholders were involved. However, the intention of the MOU was not meant to be a definitive document but a living one, based on changes and needs of each of the parties as the collaboration was sustained and built upon.

With the groundwork laid, we had discussions about how to develop the collaboration and how we could further embed the philosophical basis of the project, that of enhancing student learning. For the partnership to progress smoothly, we discussed each department's motives, goals and visions, and set guidelines in order to ensure that the collaboration would be put into practice effectively.

We began by defining trade jargon within our respective professions. We all understand that every profession has its own set of trade jargon; librarians often talk about 'information literacy' and Residence Life about 'high-impact practices'. Without a shared understanding of such terms, working with each other could have been difficult. Throughout all of our conversations, we maintained a keen awareness of our use of jargon, ensuring that we explained all terms to each other to enable us to develop a common vocabulary. Because both parties were focused on enhancing student learning as a shared philosophy, we knew we needed to share a common language, so we developed a group of shared definitions, especially in regards to spaces and their purpose. For example, the building had a room meant for faculty to meet with students before or after class, for holding office hours, or for prepping for courses. Together we named the room and developed a definition and policies for the use of this particular space.

We also had less formal discussions about our specific roles and, as a result, developed programmatic initiatives that would meet everyone's goals. Although we both understood that we each had other job responsibilities, we wanted to develop a plan that would ensure that we could support one another within the context of each person's position. For example, the librarian was responsible for outreach to the residential community. As a way to support these outreach efforts, the Residence Life coordinator was responsible for communicating these initiatives to the staff of resident assistants in the building, as well as sharing with other professional staff and a wider array of students when appropriate. It was also decided that both parties should be present to support the other's events. For example the librarian, in collaboration with the resident scholar, held an 'Open House' in the library space early in the academic year. The Residence Life coordinator attended this event, and required student staff to attend with their residents as well. The librarian also agreed to be present for Residence Life events such as move-in day, and the opening meeting that all residents were required to attend.

Sustaining and building upon the collaboration

- Be aware of departmental goal changes through continued conversations about activities in each department, and in the wider field.

- Sustain the collaboration as you would any other relationship (professional or personal) by giving it the attention that it needs.
- Approach the collaboration with an open mind, understand strengths and areas of growth and make adjustments as necessary.

After initial discussions, we developed strategies for how to build and sustain our collaboration. We scheduled regular meetings in which we engaged in information sharing, brainstorming, and giving each other feedback.

This was a time for both parties to be cognizant of departmental activities and goals as well as potential changes which could have an impact on continuing the partnership. For example, the Residence Life coordinator kept the librarian up to date on changes to the model that Residence Life used to interact with residents, and the electronic dashboard that they used to connect with students. Managerial pressures were at play in this example; Residence Life was responding to an external driver to ensure that they were meeting students' needs for information in the most technologically appropriate way. This information might inform the librarian's interactions with residents as well. To learn more about the field, the librarian and the Residence Life coordinator attended conferences and training events intended for the opposite department. For example, the librarian was part of the resident assistant training, and the Residence Life coordinator attended a local library conference. Additionally, we frequently used each other's expertise to plan academic experiences or when confronted with a student issue or question we were unable to address. The librarian used the Residence Life coordinator's knowledge about student development to help guide some of the book collection acquisition, and the librarian supported the Residence Life coordinator with understanding how students can contribute to the scholarly conversation through undergraduate research opportunities.

The ability to sustain and build upon a collaboration requires similar traits to building and sustaining a personal relationship: we needed to pay attention, to demonstrate our interest, and to respond appropriately. One strategy was to ensure that no matter how busy our schedules got and despite the availability of email (which we also used), we would make an effort to meet face-to-face regularly to ensure that the needs of both departments were being met, and to develop a collegial and supportive environment. Our efforts to meet weekly allowed us to return to our philosophical motivation for our relationship, namely to enhance student learning. We also sought opportunities to meet outside of the work context in order to gain a better understanding of each other, and to develop a trusting relationship.

Supporting each other required us to approach the collaboration with an open mind. This was especially crucial since neither of us had experience with creating and developing a residence hall library, or with working in a residence hall with such a large number of academic programs and stakeholders. Whenever we had an idea for a new initiative, we kept an open mind and were willing to try out ideas for new initiatives, especially if they met both of the departments' goals. For example, the librarian served as an embedded librarian within a class associated with one of the academic programs that was housed in their shared space. This allowed the librarian to be present in a space that felt to students both academic and comfortable. This particular class focused on undergraduate research and was taught by one of the building's resident assistants who managed the floor upon which his students lived. This model allowed students to truly feel a connection between their curricular and co-curricular experience, and to see the librarian as a resource and familiar face when they needed assistance later in the year.

Having an open mind also means being open to feedback, and allowing each of the partners to contribute to the project. If one partner approaches the other with a fully developed plan already in place, it may not allow both parties to feel like they have a stake in the project through a specific contribution. This lack of contributory investment could lead to problems that undermine the participants' shared philosophy; in this case, that of enhancing student learning. For contributions to be meaningful and successful, both partners should be aware of what the other brings to the project or goal (Swartz, Carlisle, and Uyeki, 2006) and be open to discussion. Tools such as StrengthsQuest can be used to aid understanding of each other's strengths and areas of growth. Although we did not formally take a StrengthsQuest test together, we had both previously completed them in separate contexts; we shared our results to gain a better understanding of each other's strengths. Additionally, through working collaboratively we naturally began to understand each other's strengths and areas of growth, and adapt to them. For example, the librarian had strong graphic design skills, so she often created advertising for shared programming.

Facing challenges

- Discuss challenges and be aware of the political landscape/philosophies of departmental leaders.
- Assess the partnership on an ongoing basis to ensure individual and group goals are being met.

Understanding and being aware of university politics and the politics of the departments could help to ease some of the challenges that collaborations can face, especially if the project is coming from the administration; departmental goals can change as the partnership develops and grows. Although it may not always be in the foreground, keeping good political relationships by not stepping on each other's toes and by building consensus can have a big impact on how well the groups work and grow with one another. There is bound to be some confusion whenever two large departments enter into a collaboration, especially on issues of logistics and politics. Because the librarian at UO was housed within a University Housing space, she had to learn certain ways to go about making requests for facility and other space-related issues. For example, the librarian wanted to host an event in which therapy dogs would come to the library space during final exams. Though the space 'belonged' to the Libraries, she had to ensure that Housing agreed to the event (they did!).

It was sometimes a challenge for those 'on the ground' in the collaboration to understand the various policies of the other department. To mitigate this effect, both departments made sure to share relevant contact information with the other whenever possible.

While facilities issues surfaced most often, confusion also arose in relation to financial decision-making. This sometimes became complicated when decisions regarding funding needed to be made quickly, especially since it was often not the base level collaborators (us) who had access to financial data and decision making authority. When financial issues surfaced, we referred back to the MOU as well as having conversations with our departments' administrative teams and scheduling meetings with those who could make financial decisions, to determine how the finances should be handled.

Although these issues never inhibited the two departments from accomplishing their goals, it should be noted that they may surface in new partnerships. These challenges also served as a reminder that, while we were focused on student learning as the reason for our partnership, others above us may have had more managerial-based reasoning.

Assessment is very important for sustaining and building collaborations. Not knowing if the goals of the individual departments and collective goals were being met, we did not know if we were working well together. Individually and collaboratively, the two departments wanted to know more about students' attitudes and experiences with the academic programs and with the library space. In the spring of 2013, the librarian held a focus group session and in spring 2014, Residence Life conducted a survey of students housed in the academic programs that included questions developed collaboratively about usage of the Library Commons space, collection and services. All of the information collected helped us to understand which goals the individual departments were not reaching, which collaborative goals were being met, and how we could help each other to achieve outcomes that were not being met. Not only did the departments benefit from the assessment of the partnership; the students did too.

With a well-developed partnership that ran smoothly and seamlessly, there were more opportunities to focus on developing learning opportunities for students beyond the classroom. For example in 2013, the Libraries further collaborated with Residence Life to reach other populations of students, such as sophomores in the Sophomore Year Experience hall.

Conclusion

Departments of residence life and university libraries both seek to support student academic experiences and success at a university, though their methods may be different. Residence life professionals often look to student development theory, knowing that it can be challenging for a student to succeed in a class if they do not feel part of the campus community. Librarians might focus on information literacy, and providing research tools essential for student academic success. In either case, both units are working to provide students with the necessary skills to succeed in the face of a difficult roommate situation, a confusing paper topic, or going to faculty office hours for the first time. It is through this shared philosophical focus on student learning that we have found success in creating an effective collaboration.

For those who do library outreach, the value in collaborating with residence life staff is clear: at most institutions, they are in close contact with a great number of students, especially those in their first year. Residence life staff understand the academic conditions and stresses that students face outside of the classroom, and recognize that libraries can be a significant source of support. As a result, librarians have partnered with Residence Life staff at the University of Oregon to bring information literacy and research to the halls. Residence Life also has much to gain from this partnership. There is a growing trend across this field to support students' in-class experiences by creating opportunities for students to integrate their academic work into co-curricular settings. Many residence life departments partner with academic units to develop living-learning communities that blend student living and learning experiences.

Library support in the development of these communities, as well as the invaluable resources that librarians can provide for students, create the need for this collaborative partnership.

What started out as a partnership between the University of Oregon Libraries and University Housing and Residence Life to locate a library in a residence hall has benefited the work of both departments, the students, and those individuals involved in sustaining the collaboration. Through this partnership we have raised awareness of the activities of each of the departments. This has allowed us to share the same student-centred vision for supporting students, staff and faculty in the residence halls; to avoid duplication of work; and to grow our departmental goals. For us as individual collaborators, it has been a personal and professional development opportunity that has enabled us to use the knowledge we learned from each other to inform the work that we do. As a result, the students benefitted the most from the collaboration: our work has created an integrated academic and residential living experience that focuses on student learning as the catalyst to help them develop personally and academically for future success.

References

Association of College & Research Libraries. 2015. *Framework for information literacy in higher education*. [Online]. [Accessed 8 September 2015]. Available from: http://www.ala.org/acrl/standards/ilframework

Kezar, A. 2001. Documenting the landscape: results of a national study on academic and student affairs collaborations. *New Directions for Higher Education*. [Online]. **2001**(116), pp.39–52. [Accessed 10 August 2014]. Available from: http://onlinelibrary.wiley.com

Kraemer, E., Keyse, D.J. and Lombardo, S.V.l. 2003. Beyond these walls: building a library outreach program at Oakland University. *The Reference Librarian*. 82, pp.5-17.

Kuh, G.D. 2008. High-impact educational practices: What they are, who has access to them, and why they matter. Washington, DC: Association of American Colleges and Universities.

Pascarella, E.T. and Terenzini, P.T. 2005. *How college affects students: a third decade of research*. San Francisco: Jossey-Bass Publishers.

National Survey of Student Engagement. 2014. *About NSSE, 2014.* [Online]. [Accessed 24 August 2014]. Available from http://nsse.iub.edu/html/about.cfm

Swartz, P.S., Carlisle, B.A. and Chisato Uyeko, E. 2006. Libraries and student affairs: partners for student success. *Reference Services Review.* **35**(1), pp.109-122.

A tale of three cities: an interprofessional, inter-institutional collaboration

By Michelle Schneider and Jade Kelsall

About the authors

Michelle Schneider is a Learning Advisor at Leeds University Library, supporting taught students to develop their academic and information literacies. She is an Associate Fellow of the Higher Education Academy and has recently been awarded a developmental University Student Education Fellowship from the University of Leeds. Michelle has been involved on a national level with both learning development and information literacy: she is a member of the ALDinHE Professional Development Working Group, she co-judged the 2015 CREDO Reference Award and was Runner up Information Literacy Practitioner of the Year in 2013.

Jade is an independent blended learning consultant specialising in instructional design and online course development. Prior to going solo she worked as a learning technologist in higher education libraries, most recently at the University of Manchester Library where she was involved in the development of the award-winning My Learning Essentials programme. She continues to work closely with colleagues in higher education sector, and remains active in the library world through her work with the CoPILOT committee and on the CILIP Information Literacy Groups website editorial team. In 2014, Jade was runner up in the Association of Learning Technology (ALT) Learning Technologist of the Year award.

Introduction

Other chapters in this book have discussed the ways in which interprofessional collaborations can lead to more effective and integrated services for students, as well as positively impact on or in some cases even transform the practice of the professionals involved. However, they have mostly been driven by the institution, directed from the top-down rather than the bottom-up. Collaborations do not always have to occur like this. They do not have to be large scale and permanent; they can be informal, short term and with a single goal in mind. Nor does collaboration always have to be only within our own institutions; in our networked society, we have more opportunity than ever before to forge relationships across institutional and geographic boundaries.

In this chapter I will share with you an honest account of how I implemented an interprofessional, inter-institutional collaboration to create an online resource. This was the first collaborative project that I had led on and I was very naive about the entire process. I did not extensively research how to run a collaborative project (or any project for that matter) and, while the project was ultimately a success, I made numerous mistakes along the way. The aim of the chapter is to provide practical advice derived from my real experience of running this project to help you to instigate your own informal, short-term collaborations, and learn from our successes as well as our numerous mistakes.

The chapter was written collaboratively by two of the project team, though much of the narrative is told from the perspective of Michelle as the project lead.

The collaboration

The Student Guide to Social Media was a collaboratively designed online resource that aims to help any student, irrespective of institution to understand how to make use of social media to enhance the skills they need at university and beyond, including researching, networking and crafting their online identity.

The team that developed the resource was:

- Michelle Schneider, University of Leeds Library, Academic Skills Advisor (at the time of the project; now Learning Advisor). Carla Harwood (Graduate Trainee at the time of the project) assisted Michelle with various parts of the project

- Sam Aston, University of Manchester Library, Teaching and Learning Librarian

- Jade Kelsall, University of Manchester, e-Learning Technologist (at the time of the project; now an independent e-learning consultant)

- Ned Potter, University of York Library, Academic Liaison Librarian. Chris Millson from the Careers Service at York provided additional input[1].

Why an interprofessional collaboration?

The diverse spread of learning support professionals working in higher education includes librarians, learning developers, career advisors, e-learning officers, English for academic purposes advisors and disability support tutors, among others. The boundaries between the remit and roles of these professionals are often fluid, both within and across institutions.

In 2013, the ALDinHE professional development group collated a sample of job descriptions advertising for learning developers (LD) or that had an explicit LD element. The diversity of the samples collected highlighted the breadth of the roles, remits and structures that these professionals are operating in, even just within the area of learning development (ALDinHE, 2013).

---

[1] The resource is available at https://www.escholar.manchester.ac.uk/learning-objects/social-media-guide/ under a Creative Commons BY-NC license

Despite the lack of consistency across professions, we are all ultimately working towards the same goal: helping students to develop their own strategies for learning and improving their skills. Emma Coonan recently observed of librarians and learning developers that "We're all converging on the same goal: to provide opportunities for our students to construct and sensemake the academic landscape for themselves" (2014). As the lines between roles and remits become increasingly blurred, the benefits of building relationships and collaborating across these professions are clearly emerging: working in this way allows us to draw from each other's expertise, to avoid duplication of effort, and to provide the most consistent and high-quality service we can for all students entering higher education.

It was clear from early on that this project would be more successful if developed as a collaborative effort, involving colleagues who had the professional skills and expertise that I was lacking. At the time, I was working in a small team of Academic Skills Advisors. While I had the most experience and interest within my team in using social media for academic purposes, it was not my area of expertise. I also lacked the skills that I knew would be required to create a high-quality online resource, such as instructional design, visual design and e-learning development. I therefore set about identifying suitable collaborative partners who would bring the right professional experience and expertise to the project.

Why inter-institutional?

There is an already well-established tradition of sharing ideas and resources among learning support professionals working across HE institutions. There are numerous active JISCMail lists such as LDHEN, in which learning developers exchange information, share teaching materials and discuss key issues arising in the profession. Initiatives such as CoPILOT have been instrumental in encouraging library and information professionals to share their information literacy materials as open educational resources. In less formal but often more active and reactive environments such as Twitter, there is a huge amount of discussion and sharing across professions and institutions.

One of the reasons for such culture of sharing between learning support services is that we often provide similar support to our students in our respective institutions. For example, many of us provide referencing support and, while some of the specific requirements may vary, each institution will have similar requirements for teaching materials, online learning resources and written guidance. Sharing such materials allows for less duplication of effort.

There is additional value in taking this sharing culture one step further by partnering with other institutions to create such materials. From an individual perspective, it gives participants the opportunity to build closer ties with colleagues that they wouldn't usually work with, learning from the expertise of the other partners. It can lead to a higher quality of the final output because it enables the materials to benefit from this collective expertise and the diverse skill sets that each partner brings. For the partner institutions, the partners can observe first-hand how colleagues working in learning support services at other universities tackle a project, providing insights into how they are structured and how they deliver their services to students. This allows each partner to learn from the successes of the others, giving them the opportunity to implement these new ideas within their own teams.

What is meant by informal?

The term 'informal' is used within this chapter because the project was not something we were instructed to embark on by our respective employers; each of the partners chose to be involved. In addition, there was no formal agreement between the institutions. While we all made a commitment to complete the project, it was not in any way formalised through a contract or other formal agreement; we did not need to put forward an official proposal, report regular progress to anyone, take minutes of our meetings or even write up a project report at the end. This is not to say that it was a renegade project without any institutional support: we all sought permission from our managers to work on the project, but it was very much led by the project team ourselves.

Instigating your own collaborative project

In the rest of this chapter, I will share my experience to illustrate how you might approach starting your own project. While some of this advice can be applied to any collaborative project, or indeed any project at all, I have focused particular attention on the specific issues that may arise from informal, interprofessional inter-institutional collaborations.

Get the right people

What is the best thing about actively seeking your own collaboration? You get to choose who you work with. When collaboration is forced on you, you often have no such luxury. For me, there were three main factors that constituted "right":

- People that bring the relevant knowledge, skills and perspectives to the project you are working on. Ensuring that everyone brings something different to the table will help to reduce the risk of disagreements as each person will have their own particular expertise or perspective to contribute.
- People you get on with and you think will get on with each other. As this project was self-driven, I was particularly keen to ensure that it would be enjoyable, and so choosing people I knew I'd get on with was important to me to avoid it becoming a chore. Think about the people you already know whom you work best with. Whom have you met at conferences or even on Twitter that you have a rapport with? Are there people you are on groups or committees with that you get on well with?
- People with similar professional values as you. This doesn't mean you need to have the same professional background; more important is the way you think about and approach your work.

For example, there has been much discussion and debate within the library profession as to whether librarians are 'teachers' or 'trainers' in the context of their role of developing students' information literacy skills (Schneider and Pullinger, 2012; Wheeler and Mckinney, 2014). There is a significant difference between those two mind-sets, so when working on a short-term collaboration it is far more beneficial to work with people who share such values, particularly when they are directly relevant to the project you are working on.

What we did successfully

Selected people for their professional expertise.

I was the lead, so my role was of a co-ordinator and project manager and I was the person who handpicked the people for the project. I chose Jade for her instructional design and e-learning development skills, Sam for her creative input and experience running a module about digital literacy and Ned for his expertise in social media and penchant for writing for different audiences.

Selected people I knew I could work with and could work with each other.

I knew Ned from his time working at the University of Leeds. He seemed quite laid back yet from his prolific online profile I could see that he would be an asset to the project and would bring valuable and real experience of using social media. Prior to her move to the University of Manchester I had worked with Jade at Leeds, during which time we'd established a very positive working relationship. She is also a good friend. While this doesn't necessarily make for a great working partnership, I knew that we had a similar work ethic and she would not mind discussing the project on evenings and weekends. Jade and Ned had also worked on a project together at Leeds; I had met Sam at several LILAC conferences, and Jade and Sam had a great working relationship since Jade had started working at the University of Manchester.

As we already knew each other reasonably well, everyone felt comfortable sharing their ideas right from the start. This did not mean we agreed on everything, but it did mean we could have honest and open conversations.

Selected people with the same professional values

From the start, I was very clear about what I didn't want to create. My professional values (derived both from my experience as a subject librarian and as an academic skills advisor) are grounded in a belief in empowering students in their learning, rather than giving them a prescriptive set of rules to follow. I did not want to create a training guide for students on using social media; I wanted to make students think about how they could use social media to enhance their academic work and ultimately gain valuable skills that would help them beyond their university life. I did not want to provide a written guide of the dos and donts of using social media; I wanted to help students to make their own decisions about if, when and how to use social media, and provide tips on making the most of the available tools.

I was fairly certain that Sam, Jade and Ned would want to take a similar approach. Sam had been delivering a module about 'The Digital Society' at Manchester; the assessment gave students the chance to work in groups undertaking a project for a real-life client, which required the students to use their initiative, work independently and take responsibility for their decisions. I had worked with Jade already and knew we had similar professional values. It was clear from Ned's blog that he shared my focus on student learning and adopting a variety of teaching methods to engage the students in their learning (Potter, 2012).

What we could have done:

In my case, I quickly decided on who I wanted to work on the project with, and luckily they all said yes. However, there are alternative means of sourcing your project team if your potential collaborators don't immediately jump out at you.

Put a call out for collaborators. Find out where conversations are taking place about the area that you are working on, then get involved with them. Consider all possible networks including relevant mailing lists (JISCMail is a good place to start), social media networks and blogs. Ask your colleagues for suggestions.

Depending on the nature of your project, you might consider looking for collaborators in other sectors such as further education, schools, health or public libraries.

When putting out a call, make it clear what you are looking for. Include as much information as you can that will help your potential collaborators to understand what you want to do, what they will get out of it and what you'll need from them.

- What do you want to achieve with this project? If you do not have a definite output in mind, describe in general terms what you wish to work on.
- What are you looking for in a collaborator? What skills, experience and background do you want your partners to bring to the table?
- Do you have any timescales in mind for completing the project? What are they, and how strict are your deadlines?
- How much time do you envisage your partners needing to contribute?

If you are unclear yourself about any of these questions, you can still initiate a collaboration; the scope of the project can be decided between you when you have your group together. It might be useful to ask your potential collaborators to write a short pitch, outlining why they want to be involved in the project and what they think they will bring to it. This will help you decide who might be a best 'fit', particularly if you're lucky enough to generate a lot of interest.

Partnerships can begin more organically than this. Conferences and other events are potential opportunities to meet people who are on the same professional page as you, with similar interests and values. As well as being useful to building your professional network, these serendipitous meetings can also be fertile ground from which to grow a collaborative relationship.

Define what you are trying to achieve

This may seem obvious but it's important to not just agree on an eventual output but to also consider what the underlying aim of the collaboration is. The ultimate output may flexible as there are usually a number of different approaches that can be taken to achieve a particular goal.

The key to an effective and enjoyable collaboration is that you all agree on this. For example, the goal of a project might be to help new undergraduate students develop their own strategies to manage their time. The output could be many things: online tutorial, a video, a set of teaching materials to be used with students in their own institutions. Agreeing on the underlying goal will help you to decide on what outputs you will need to best to achieve that goal. Whatever outputs you decide on, further decisions will have to be made along the way; each of these decisions should be measured against how it contributes to achieving that goal or not.

In addition, you may want to consider what you want to achieve from collaborative working itself. Are there benefits that you want to see from working in this way as opposed to working as individuals or just within your institutions, and if so, how will you evidence them?

What we did successfully

Agreed a unifying goal

We had a face-to-face project kick-off meeting, which was a great opportunity to have an open discussion about what we wanted to achieve, and to generate lots of ideas. I shared my vision with the team and we all agreed on our unifying goal for the project: this was to be a student-centred resource and to us that meant including the student voice where possible, empowering the student to make their own decisions and ensuring the tone, content and aesthetics would be developed with only a student audience in mind. Every decision we made about the resource was based on whether it met these goals.

To illustrate, at the first meeting we considered how we were going to make sure this wasn't a training resource telling students how to use social media. The first thing we agreed was that to achieve this goal, the resource would need to be task-driven rather than tool-driven. For example, instead of the student coming to the resource and looking at a section about Twitter, we wanted them to think about what they were trying to achieve, such as crafting their online identity. This would then introduce them to the different tools they could use to achieve this goal, one of which would be Twitter. However, we also thought that some students may be looking directly for information about how to make the best use of a specific tool. We thus agreed that would provide two ways into the resource: task or tool. We knew that this would make the structure of the resource considerably more complex and that it would require a lot more work in both planning and development than if it were simply structured around the tool. However, we had all agreed that we needed to put student needs first, so we had to make it happen (and we did).

What we should have done differently

Define clearly what success of collaborative working would look like:

We had established what short-term success looked like: creating the online resource. However, we had no plan as to how we would evaluate the impact of the resource, and therefore no way to prove that the collaboration was a success apart from the anecdotal evidence we received and our own feelings about it. As with any project, it is important to decide how you are going to measure the impact of your work: how will you know whether your ultimate goal has been achieved?

We also did not consider how we could demonstrate the specific benefit of undertaking this as a collaborative project. In some ways this was because we wanted to keep this project fairly informal and focused on the one goal; we had a very specific aim in mind and were not looking at the potential for longer-term collaborative working. In hindsight this was a missed opportunity to establish more collaborative projects and encourage our colleagues to do the same.

Establish roles and responsibilities

Try to establish some distinctive roles within a collaborative project, though they need not be too rigid. In an inter-professional collaboration, people will generally be involved because of their particular expertise or experience (technical, subject, pedagogical, create etc.), so some element of their role within the project is likely to be clear from the outset, but individuals also have other talents and abilities that can emerge over time and these should be given space to emerge.

The one role that needs to be established from the start is project manager. Sometimes we can shy away from establishing any type of hierarchy in collaborative projects for fear of seeming undemocratic but without having an individual assigned the role of project manager, deadlines can pass without anyone taking overall responsibility for driving the project forward. They can also have a broad overview of what everyone is doing, keep an eye on the bigger picture, keep everyone informed of what is happening, be a central point of contact and assign tasks based on availability, ability and priority.

What we did successfully

Established a project manager

It made sense for me as the person who instigated the project to be the project manager. Also, my institution was expecting me to produce something, so the project was a higher priority for me than it was for the other partners, thus I was the most likely to keep the project on track and push it forward. This was agreed by the whole group.

Allowed people's roles to develop organically

While people were brought into the project due to their professional abilities, roles were not set in stone from the start (aside from Jade who would be responsible for building the resource, and me who would manage the project). Individuals will often have skills and strengths that are not immediately apparent if they don't use them in their daily job, or if you don't work with them on a regular basis.

Our approach to content writing is an apt illustration of this. At the first meeting we all agreed to go away and write a section of the content. The rationale behind this was that we would independently write the section in the way we envisaged it should be and then bring them together, taking the best bits of each to create a template that we had all contributed to in order to complete the rest of the content. This worked well for several reasons: it was democratic as it was not just the most assertive in the group that could get their way; it was time-efficient as four of the sections would have been started straight away, and it was easier to work on something concrete from the start, rather than attempting to agree on what was still a fairly abstract concept at that point. This process revealed some very clear strengths. For example, Ned showed a particular aptitude for writing for a student audience and so it was agreed that he would be the final editor of the written content to ensure a consistency of tone and language.

What you could do

Define roles from the outset

A different approach that may have been more efficient would have been to identify what needed to be done as part of the project, define what skills would be needed for each task, ask each partner to outline their own particular strengths and interests, and allocate the work accordingly.

Create a project plan

As already discussed, a project manager is essential, but it is also important to establish collectively how a project is going to run, though it may change over the duration of the project. This is particularly necessary if you are working with people from different institutional or geographical locations. The key things that should be decided upon are:

- channels of communication
- frequency of meetings (both virtual and online)
- how work will be produced and shared
- deadlines and timescales
- dissemination strategy (if applicable)

What we did successfully

Agreed on channels of communication

We had one face-to-face meeting at the start of the project (only two in total). We all lived and worked in different cities, so regular face-to-face meetings were neither time nor cost efficient. We felt that an in-person meeting at the start was important to establish initial relationships, generate initial ideas, agree communication channels etc., but that as far as possible we would communicate virtually for the duration of the project.

We agreed to use the following tools:

- Google Drive for a shared space to save all of our content documents and collate our ideas
- Skype for virtual meetings
- Email for general communication and updates

Built in contingency time from the start

With colleagues from three different institutions involved, we knew that we were likely to have competing priorities. This can be a particular issue with more informal collaborative projects as the project can often go to the bottom of the priorities list. Although I had been tasked with this activity by my institution, I wasn't given a final deadline and for the rest of the project team this was in addition to their day-to-day workload. Indeed, conflicting priorities both work and personal meant that at times people (including myself) went quiet on the project. In the initial meeting has we agreed on two deadlines for the project: a realistic ideal deadline and a 'by the absolute latest' date. This gave us some contingency time and took the pressure off.

Took a pragmatic approach to decision-making

As the project progressed it was clear that it was neither possible nor necessary for everyone to be actively involved at every stage of the project or with every decision. This actually made things easier at times, as not every small decision had to be agonised over by all of the project partners. For example, Jade and I had a lot of discussion (and disagreement) over the visual design of the resource. A number of versions went back and forth until we came up with a compromise we were both happy with; this then went to everyone else for final comments and approval. To have had everyone involved in reviewing each version of the design would have slowed things down at a time that we wanted to get on with the development of the resource; as it was, we were able to get the design almost finalised within a few hours, rather than days.

Ultimately as long as everyone completes their set tasks and the project team is kept informed and given a chance to object to any final decisions, it can be beneficial for a smaller faction of the group to move forward with certain parts of the project without needed to seek input from the whole team at every turn.

What we should have done

Create a formal work plan with intermediate deadlines for the project.

As project manager, this should have been something I did but I didn't. This was a mistake as it meant a lot of chasing up and deadlines being set on an ad hoc basis. I would update people via email rather than using a central, progress document; looking back, this now seems like a ridiculous way to run a project! This meant that people got overwhelmed with emails and it was hard to stay on track with the project. I also ended up meeting up separately with colleagues on the project to establish where we were up to and what they still needed to do. This probably would not have been necessary if I had created a more robust project plan.

In addition, some complete honesty here. As Jade and I were very good friends, when things fell behind we would often meet up at evenings and weekends to finish work off. This is not necessarily desirable or even possible for most people, so setting clear, achievable deadlines is extremely important.

I should also highlight that in this case, while we did have a deadline for the project it was a fairly arbitrary one. If we had not managed to complete the project on time it wouldn't have caused any real problems, so when the project timeline slipped we didn't need to worry about it too much. If we had had a hard deadline, we would have needed to have formalised the planning process in order to ensure we completed on time.

Book regular meetings

It would have been a good idea to book in regular catch-up meetings right from the start. It can be difficult to stay in touch with people working at a distance; you can't just pop into the office next door to discuss issues as they arise, and working in different locations means that you are often less aware of the broader context in which your partners are working, such as when they're away from the office, what their other priorities are and how heavy their workload is. I tried to arrange Skype meetings on an ad hoc basis when I felt we needed a catch up, but this was often difficult as people were on annual leave or away at conferences at different times. This was not time efficient and sometimes meant elements of the project fell behind while I was awaiting responses from the team.

Develop a dissemination strategy.

The benefit of interprofessional and inter-institutional collaboration is that each person has access to different networks, allowing you to disseminate the work you are doing to a wider audience then may have been previously been possible. We failed to develop a strategy that would make the best of our various connections and networks; indeed, we didn't even consider it until we had completed the project. Once we had finished the resource, we disseminated the finished project across various mailing lists (LHDEN, LIS-INFOLIT), social media and presented it at a few conferences. This was done in an ad-hoc way and we by no means had a strategy. This was a missed opportunity to make the most of the collaboration.

Identify specific challenges of inter-institutional collaboration

Working collaboratively across institutions can bring its own challenges, even in informal partnerships such as this. Differences in procedure, student demographic, administration, identities and institutional cultures can all present potential barriers to effective collaborative working. These barriers are not necessarily insurmountable, though you will benefit from trying to predict what issues may arise early on in your project so that you can consider how to approach reaching a workable solution for all parties.

From the outset, you need to be clear that there is enough alignment of your goals to make a collaboration between institutions feasible. If your core goals and values are not sufficiently matched; if the nature of the project is not broad enough to be equally beneficial to all parties; or if the priorities and deadlines of each partner are not parallel, then it may be that the project is not appropriate for committing to an inter-institutional collaboration.

What we did successfully

Predicted branding issues

One of the main issues we had was the branding of the online resource, which is a challenge likely to present itself in many projects with an external-facing output.

Two of the three partner institutions had well-established brands for their online learning resources, both of which had distinctive visual identities. The team discussed the idea of creating three versions of the same resource, each of which would be branded appropriately for each institution. We all agreed that this was not an ideal situation; not only would it create more work and reduce the sustainability of the resource by having to maintain three separate versions, but it also would undermine the ethos of the collaborative project.

We all discussed this with our respective institutions; two of the three were happy for us to create our own design for the resource without needing to adhere to either institution's visual identify guidelines. The third was concerned about the resource not being strongly identified as part of the existing suite of learning resources, and wanted us to use the same branding as the other resources. After considering this for a while, we came up with an amicable compromise: we would stick with one version of the resource in our own design, but create a landing page linking to it that had the appropriate institutional branding. It then wouldn't look out of place amongst the others on their website, but we avoided having the issue of three separate versions to maintain.

Balanced our institution-specific issues with our main goal

A discussion arose early on about whether to include LinkedIn in the guide. At my institution, advice and guidance on LinkedIn is provided by the Careers Centre so I was cautious not to step into the domain of another service. At York and Manchester however, staff involved in careers support expressed enthusiasm for the resource we were creating and wanted LinkedIn to be incorporated. As a group, we agreed that this would be important for our students and as we all agreed right at the start of the project that the priority was the student audience, it was essential that we found a way to include it. I met up with a colleague from the Careers Centre to discuss our concerns, and ultimately we found a compromise that satisfied both of our requirements: we included a sub-section on LinkedIn, and linked to the resources provided by the University of Leeds Career Centre.

What we should have done

Build in time for respective institutional approval

Each institution may have different protocols and processes for that could be relevant to your project. A typical example of this is the signing-off of any project outputs. It wasn't until we were ready to release the resource that we all realised we needed to go back to our respective institutions for approval before launch.

Consider the long-term sustainability of the project

While this collaborative project was meant to be short-term, the output was intended to have long-term impact. We did not discuss who would be responsible for the maintenance of the resource once the project had come to an end, or what would happen if one of the project team left their institution.

In our case, it was fairly clear that responsibility for the source files and making any physical changes to the resource would remain with Jade at Manchester, as she was the only member of the team who had the skills and access to the software to do so.

However, in April 2015 Jade left her post at the University of Manchester, and it was only at this point that we discussed the longer-term plan for ensuring the guide would be maintained. By this point, there was a small e-learning team at the University of Manchester Library who would be able to make any changes required to the resource in future, and as Sam remained in post at Manchester, there was no need to change our approach. Had this not been the case, the resource could have fell into disrepair quickly and easily if none of the three partner libraries had the relevant skills to be able to update it.

This is something that needs to be discussed at the start of the project; without planning for sustainability, outputs can quickly become out of date and your hard word may soon be wasted.

Conclusion

Embarking on a collaborative project that pools the expertise and experience from a number of different professions and institutions can clearly reap a number of benefits. Writing this chapter has given me a chance to reflect on my experience; with the benefit of hindsight, it is clear that we missed an opportunity to exploit the wider significance of the project.

We set out to create an online resource, and in that aim we succeeded.

However, if we had set ourselves an additional aim to use the project as an exploration of the benefits of the inter-institutional approach as a way of working, it could have become a springboard to creating longer-term working relationships with the project partners, and to further projects in partnership with other institutions.

I hope that this chapter provides the practical advice that I wish I had considered when undertaking this project, and that in learning from my mistakes and successes, you may be encouraged to instigate your own collaborative projects and use the lessons from my shared experience to implement them successfully.

References

ALDinHE. 2013. Sample of Job Descriptions. [Online]. [Date accessed 22 October 2015]. Available from: https://aldinheprofdev.wordpress.com/sharing-experience/job-descriptions-2/

Coonan, E. 2014. "My dolly's bigger than your dolly", or, why our labels no longer matter. 29 April. The Mongoose Librarian. [Online]. [Accessed 28 October 2015]. https://librariangoddess.wordpress.com/2014/04/29/my-dollys-bigger/

Potter, N. 2012. Rebooting infolit, the battle decks way. [Online]. [Accessed 27 October 2015]. Available from: http://www.ned-potter.com/blog/2046

Extra Biographical detail

John Sutter is Learning Enhancement and Support Manager at the University for the Creative Arts in Canterbury, where he leads on language and learning development. He has worked in education for over 25 years in the UK and abroad, initially as a language teacher and then as a teacher trainer and educational consultant, including seven years as part of the nationally renowned team at LLU+, London South Bank University, where among other things he developed and ran an innovative and unique MA in creative and critical teaching education. He is also a founder member of Learning Unlimited, the social enterprise that was formed to continue their work. His key interests are the politics of language, teaching as a creative art, and, in particular, improvisation and 'jazz' understandings of language and teaching - both of which dovetail with his additional activity as a musician.

Index

A
academic integrity, 108–109, 125, 126, *see also What did I do wrong?* project
academic skills, 96, 97, 118, 125
academic staff
    collaborations, 16–19, 80, 90–92, 100–101, 138–139
    embedding learning development, 45, 55, 75, 127
    perception of roles, 18, 22, 93, 113
    staff development, 49, 127–128
    as stakeholders, 110, 125, 131–132
academic writing, 83–84, 85–86, 90, 125
accommodation, *see* residential services
accountability, 18, 143, *see also* decision-making
administrative staff, 110–111
agreements, formal, 142–143, 157–158
alignment, 33–34, 61, 98, 169
analysis, 124
approval, institutional, 170–171
assessments, 87–89, 90–92
attendance, 34–35, 47–50
Australia Catholic University, 118–122
autistic spectrum conditions, 87–89
autonomy of students, 32, 34–35, 40, 43–44
away days, 63–65

B
behaviour, 39–40
branding, 169–170
Buckinghamshire New University, 57–60

C

careers, 82, 87
challenges
   as educational experience, 44
   inter-institutional, 169–172
   interprofessional, 102–105, 147–149
citations, *see* referencing
collaborations
   benefits, 126–128, 149–150
   challenges, 147–149
   post-project, 134, 171
   purpose of, 14, 16–17, 118–119, 138–139, 155–156
   research, 4–5
   theory, 14–15, 19, 20–21
collaborators
   selecting, 22–23, 65–66, 158–162
   supporting, 144, 146
collectivist approaches, 97–98
co-location, 66–67, 74, 97
communication
   with collaborators, 20–21, 24, 78–80, 144–145, 166, 168
   dissemination, 24, 110, 168–169
   with stakeholders, 22, 102–103
   with students, 35, 45–46, 67–68, 80–81
community building, 66–67, 113–114, 122–123
confidentiality, 81
consistency of guidance, 107, 126
continuing professional development (CPD), 49, 68–69, 127–132, 145, 150
credibility, 69
cross-referral, 80–81
cross-team collaboration, 90–92
culture
   on campus, 141
   professional, 97, 156–157
   team, 20, 70

curriculum-level support, 74, 90–92

D
decision-making, 143, 148, 167
design-based research (DBR), 119, 123–126
disability
   social models, 85, 91
   support, 86, 89–91
dissemination, 24, 110, 127, 168–169
dissertations, 89–92
drivers for collaborations, 138–139
dropping out, 14, 43–44, 47–48
dyslexia, 80, 85–86, 90–91

E
editing, 103, 112–113
email reminders, 45–46
embedding
   skills development, 74, 93–94, 97
   understanding of, 83–84, 127–128
employability, 63–67
empowerment, 61–62, 68–69
engagement, 14, 16, 34–35, 49, 139–140
English, inclusive, 85–86
English for Academic Purposes, 73–74, 88–89, 96, 100
enhancement, 83–84, 89
EN-MAP matrix
   background, 31–36
   need-autonomy quadrants, 37–44
   use, 44–51
Ensuring quadrant (EN-MAP), 41–42
evaluation
   of projects, 22, 24–25, 148, 163–164
   of resources, 125, 131
evidence, 21–22, 24–25, 46–47

F
finance of projects, 104, 148
flexibility
 of projects, 25
 within projects, 143, 144–145
funding of higher education, 15, 17, 47–48

G
goals
 departmental, 142, 144, 147–148
 shared, 77, 104–105, 142, 156, 162–164
 strategic, 21
government policies, 33–35

H
healthcare, collaboration in, 4–5, 14–15
higher education
 funding, 15, 17, 47–48
 participation, 41–42, 48
 policy, 33–35
 transition into, 35–36, 49, 96

I
inclusive support models, 42, 75, 85–86, 90–92
independent learners, 108, *see also* autonomy of students
informal collaborations, 154, 157–158
informal communication, 78–79, 80, 102–104, 144
information literacy, 86–87, 97, 140
inside-out factors, 33–35, 48
institutional policy, 61, 92–93, 122–123
inter-institutional collaboration, 154, 156–157, 169–172
internationalisation, 86–87
interprofessional teams
 approaches, 109
 building, 73–76, 81–82
 challenges, 102–105

J
jargon, 24, 143–144

L
language, 83–86
leadership
  cross-team, 75
  within partnership, 23–24, 122, 164–165
  values, 57–58, 60–63, 70
learning communities, 139–140, 149–150
learning development
  approaches, 83–84, 89, 97, 101
  collaborations, 63–65
  embedding, 42, 50–51
learning space, 67, 141–143
library professionals
  approaches, 97, 101, 156, 159
  collaborations, 80, 100–101, 118–119, 140–142, 148–150
  roles, 74, 120, 143–144, 159
  staff development, 128–134, 145
linguistic inclusivity, 85–86

M
managerial partnerships, 148
meetings, 81–82, 102–103, 145, 146, 168
Memoranda of Understanding, 142–143, *see also* agreements, formal
mentoring, 132–133
misconduct, 39–40, 98–99
monitoring, 47–50
Monitoring quadrant (EN-MAP), 39–40
morale, 76–78
motivation
  for collaborations, 20, 138–139
  of students, 35–36

N
networks, 109–111, 161

O
office space, 67, 78–80
online resources, 122–123, 154–155, 169–170
openness, 20, 77–78, 104, 146–147
outreach, 140–141, 148–149
outside-in factors, 33–35, 41, 47
overlapping roles, 74, 101, 155–156
overlapping roles/services, 98

P
participation in higher education, 41–42, 48
partnerships, *see* collaborations
'path-finding,' 61
personal tutors, 38
philosophies
   professional, 98, 101
   shared, 138–139, 149
plagiarism, 98–99, 108
planning, 165–169
policies
   higher education, 33–35
   organisational, 61, 92–93, 122–123
politics across university, 147
professional practice
   differences in, 105–106
   transforming, 128–129
Providing quadrant (EN-MAP), 43–44
psychometric tests, 63–64

Q
qualifications, 69, 127–128

R

reactive support, 37–38
recognition/reward, 20, 21
recruitment, 65–66
referencing, 97, 98–100, 105–108, 125
reflection, 125, 128, *see also* evaluation
relationship building, 66–67, 77–78, 104, 145–146, *see also* community building
residential services, 139–140, 141–149
Responding quadrant (EN-MAP), 37–38
restructuring, 58–61, 73–77
retention, 14, 43–44, 47–48
role models, 60–61
roles/responsibilities
   overlapping roles, 155–156
   within partnership, 23, 142–143, 144, 164–165
   understanding of, 104, 113–114, 143–144

S

selection, 65–66
'Self-Assessment Toolkit,' 18–19, 26
self-referral, 38
servant leadership, 57–58, 60
service, 57–58, 122–123
service delivery, 62
short-term projects, 154
signposting support, 74
social media, 67–68, 154, 170
socially-situated models, 83–87, 90–91
space
   learning, 67, 141–143
   office, 67, 78–80
   'third space,' 17–18, 33
staff development, 49, 68–69, 127–132, 145, 150
staff identities, 17–18

stakeholders
  engaging, 22, 110, 123–124
  identifying, 100–101, 161–162, 170
strategic support, 20–21
student ambassadors, 65–66
student experience, 15–16
student needs, *see also* EN-MAP matrix
  perceptions of, 34–35
  service delivery, 62, 85
student support, historical context, 32–35
student-focused approach, 63–66
success of collaborative projects, 20–26, 113–114, 159–172
surveys, 111
sustainability of projects, 20, 25, 144–147, 171

T
targeted support models, 42
teaching methods, 128–130
temp staff agency, 65–66
terminology, 24, 143–144
text messages, 35
theories of learning support, 83–85
'third space,' 17–18, 33
time management
  within partnership, 166–168
  of students, 35, 45–46, 108
transition into higher education, 35–36, 49, 53, 96

U
University for the Creative Arts (UCA), 73–76

V
validations, 93–94
values-driven approaches, 59–66, 68–70
vision and values, 60–61, 68–70, 77, 104–105, 160

W
What did I do wrong? project
   challenges, 102–105
   outcomes, 111–114
   overview, 99–101
   research, 105–111
widening participation, 41–42, 48
wikis, 103
working relationships, 17, 159–160
writing
   academic, 83–84, 85–86, 90, 125
   collaborative, 103, 112–113